Authentic Communication

20 CONCRETE PRACTICES TO ENHANCE YOUR COMMUNICATION & JOY

Your Communication Workbook

2ND EDITION

WORK WISDOM

KEDREN CROSBY, MPS

SARAH COLANTONIO, MS

Dedication

To all of our teammates (authentic and inauthentic).
Thank you for teaching us what matters most.

Table of contents

Letter to you, the Reader

This whole thing took shape on a road trip. On the way out to Western Pennsylvania, we worked up the list of practices to help people communicate authentically. After years of learning and teaching this stuff, we figured, let's make this easier for those who want to know more. Then we wrote the dang thing.

We get to work with such brilliant people in a myriad of organizations from non-profit to global corporations and everywhere we find wonderful human beings who find themselves struggling with the challenge of communicating. Connecting with others in a way that helps move the team to be the most innovative, creative team they can possibly be is tricky.

Maybe your organization has a noble mission to help people and yet the CEO seems to have their own agenda? Or maybe the team works really well together for the most part except when it comes to execution and then it falls apart? Or perhaps power struggles and half-truths and any number of mismanaged conflicts derail an otherwise effective team?

Authentic Communication uses methods from the field of communication and psychology to help manage many of those difficult issues. It gives language to explain what is happening so it can be worked through. These practices are concrete, so they can be intentionally implemented to help heal organizational pain OR they are useful in avoiding the kind of destructive conflicts that ruin teams and undermine the organization's effectiveness.

For example, one organization had a huge problem with what is known in family therapy as "triangulation'. Triangulation is when, instead of directly negotiating an issue with the person you are having a problem with, you go around them and talk behind their back about it. Authentic Communication teaches "non-triangulation", or a practice of first going to the person and addressing the problem with them. Once the people in the organization had language to describe what was happening, they could circumvent it by saying, "Hey wait, we decided to practice non-triangulation here. You should talk to them about this, not me."

Learning about how to manage conflict is also invaluable. It's like turning the light on in a dark room, finally you can navigate freely when you know what you're dealing with.

We hope you keep this workbook on your desk. Write all over it. Doodle in it. Go back to it. Give copies to partners, colleagues or friends. Go through it once and go through it again. Draw squiggles on the pictures. Have fun with it. Experiment. Watch your outcomes improve and then experiment some more.

ACTIVITY!

Color the picture to the right of the United States Postal Service worker and the hip Googlers below.

The reason we have them here together is they both have come to learn the immense value of **Authentic Communication** in the workplace, and they learned it in vastly different ways.

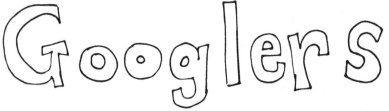

Introduction

THE PHRASE "GOING POSTAL" became part of our lexicon when an unusually high number of postal workers were involved in violent acts of mass murder, shooting their bosses, fellow workers, or even innocent bystanders. Congress directed the Postmaster General to do something about it. One of the most significant interventions was called "Project Redress."

Much of the workplace frustration had to do with communication. The culture was built on the communication style of the military. The communication patterns often looked like managers barking orders or even using intimidation

techniques to convey the urgency of a task. Little effort was expended to build rapport with interpersonal relationships. While those techniques might work for communicating in the military, they didn't work so well because the Postal Service was made up mostly of civilians.

Initially, "Project Redress" was piloted in Florida where they worked to create communication patterns and practices that would help management and employees seek to understand each other's ultimate interests, to collaborate, and become less autocratic. In other words, Authentic Communication! It was so successful that it was replicated throughout the country. Not only did it save a lot of organizational pain and suffering but it was quickly found to be a big money-saver as well. The well-being of the employees improved along with retention. The Postal Service learned about Authentic Communication but they learned about it the hard way.

In contrast, Google wanted to find out why some of their teams were so high performing

To learn more about this, search online for the article on Google in the New York Times called *"What Google Learned From Its Quest to Build the Perfect Team."*

Welcome to Your Communication Workbook and the 20 communication practices to transform your workplace. Timing is everything. This workbook is designed to be absorbed slowly, to give enough attention and space to each practice. As you work through each section, you will be able to reflect on the lessons to determine what will work best for you and the people in your organization. Be deliberate as you go through the chapters. The material we are sharing here will be transformative if put into action.

compared to others. They were made up of highly skilled, intelligent people. What was going on?

At first, when they sliced and diced the data, they couldn't figure out the secret sauce. They looked at age, sex, education but failed to see a connection. They looked at skills and even personality traits. They looked at leadership types and how well the team members knew one another. Dissecting the inner workings of 180 teams nationwide, they couldn't see a clear pattern. Yale researchers came along to help Google do some more digging.

Eventually they discovered the hidden treasures that differentiated exceptional teams from less extraordinary teams. The ingredients? Conversational turn taking was crucial. That meant team members contributed roughly the same amount of talking time. Empathy was another key ingredient. High social sensitivity, or the ability to read what is going on with another person based on their nonverbal communication, was yet another. Ultimately, they found that by creating teams where there is the ability to feel

safe, psychologically, they had better outcomes. They had more creative ideas. They had better rates of execution and they actually enjoyed working with each other. According to the author, Charles Duhigg,

"What Project Aristotle has taught people within Google is that no one wants to put on a 'work face' when they get to the office. No one wants to leave part of their personality and inner life at home. But to be fully present at work, to feel 'psychologically safe' we must know that we can be free enough, sometimes, to share the things that scare us without fear of recriminations. We must be able to talk about what is messy or sad, to have hard conversations with colleagues who are driving us crazy. We can't be focused just on efficiency. Rather, when we start the morning by collaborating with a team of engineers and then send emails to our marketing colleagues and then jump on a conference call, we want to know that those people really hear us. We want to know that work is more than just labor."

Google discovered the magic of Authentic Communication in the Google-data way.

DEFINITION:
Authentic Communication is the artful practice of building productive, trustworthy and helpful exchanges through concrete practices to foster trust and enhance the performance of teams.

The Authentic Communication practices were culled from our research and experience in family therapy, Appreciative Inquiry, psychology and communication. **Mindful Communication, Emotionally Intelligent Communication, Psychologically Safe Communication** and **Collaborative Communication** are the four dimensions of Authentic Communication.

The Four Dimensions of Authentic Communication

The environment was inherently dangerous. It was an oil rig. The biggest. And with new technology and newer projects coming up, Rick Fox was worried. While injury and death were the norm, would that be sustainable going forward? The culture of the oil rig was toughness above all else. If you didn't know how to do something, you didn't ask. Or if your buddy was killed in an accident, you soldiered on and went right back to work. Fox met Claire Nuer who persuaded him to explore something oil rig workers weren't used to exploring. Their emotions. When workers were given the opportunity to explore their feelings and become more vulnerable, to talk about what they were going through, the rate of accidents and deaths dropped dramatically.

NPR writer, Angus Chen writes in his article, "Invisibilia: How Learning to Be Vulnerable Can Make Life Safer"

"...the men had changed. By allowing themselves to become vulnerable to one another, they had altered 'their sense of who they were and could be as men...the men became more open with their feelings, other communication was starting to flow more freely.' Part of safety in an environment like that is being able to admit mistakes and being open to learning—to say, 'I need help, I can't lift this thing by myself, I'm not sure how to read this meter,' That alone is about being vulnerable.

That helped contribute to an 84 percent decline in Shell's accident rate companywide, [Robin] Elym a respected researcher reported. "In that same period, the company's level of productivity in terms of numbers of barrels and efficiency and reliability exceeded the industry's previous benchmark."

It's a powerful example of the impact of open and Authentic Communication. But even if your job requires a lot of sitting, individuals and teams uncover their original resourcefulness and creativity when communication is congruent, empathetic, conversational and self-regulated.

❶ First, **Mindful Communication:** Leaders spend 85% of their time communicating but they only absorb about 25% of what they hear. The result? Organizational pain. When relationships lack authenticity, clarity, and meaningful engagement, work is a nightmare. Relationships fall apart, projects fail, people get run down and unhappy.

Mindful Communication is reliant on deep awareness. It improves our focus and clarity in our work. While work can be a source of major stress, in the book by David Gelles called *Mindful Work,* he notes the outcome of one corporate executive's experience with mindfulness training,

> "*Employees felt more comfortable with themselves at work, more likely to pay full attention, prioritize tasks, get rid of unproductive activities, more focused overall, and self-aware. They reported dramatic spikes in their ability to 'focus on a project from beginning to end', be 'fully attentive in meetings, conference calls, and presentations,' and to 'notice when my attention has been pulled away and redirect it to the present.'*"

In our distracting world, learning how to pay attention is vital.

In the mindful communication section, you will investigate **5 concrete practices that help foster mindful communication in your workplace.** Side note, none of these practices require a meditation pillow.

❷ Secondly, **Emotionally Intelligent Communication** is communication that more often than not, predicts our success at work. If you stop and think of the best boss you've ever had, the thing that made them so great was likely related to emotional intelligence.

Emotionally Intelligent communication leverages emotional and social skills to enrich our exchanges. Emotional intelligence is how we perceive and express ourselves, how we build and maintain interpersonal relationships, how we cope with stress and use emotional data to solve problems and make decisions. Now the optimistic thing is, EI is developable. Since only about 6% of our professional success is attributable to IQ but 60-85% is directly linked to EI, it's worth investigating. It's a concrete way to invest in 'psychological capital' which, according to Dr. Fred Luthans, the father of Positive Organizational Behavior, can have up to a 200% ROI.

Increasingly, EI is being used to improve and increase performance and outcomes for many industries including health care systems, engineering, finance, tech, and education. EQs are measurements of EI and can assess individuals or teams and recommend means of improving the performance of the individual, the team, the

organization and the patient. EI is also used as a method for identifying leadership potential among team members and is increasingly used in hiring decisions.

You will explore **5 practices that help your communication be more emotionally intelligent** in this section.

❸ Thirdly, **Psychologically Safe Communication** is communication that builds safety for interpersonal risk-taking. In psychologically safe teams, members feel accepted and respected. As we mentioned earlier, Google's Project Aristotle research on effective teams found that psycholog-

ical safety was the differentiator in terms of defining what made a team most effective in problem solving and innovation. It makes sense. If you feel accepted among your team members, you can risk suggesting a weird idea knowing you won't get shot down. Making a mistake doesn't result in punishment. Questioning authority, especially if they are making a mistake, is possible.

In this section, you will learn **practices to enhance psychologically safety for yourself and your coworkers.**

❹ Lastly, the **Collaborative Communication** practices are designed to harness the collective brilliance of a group or system. Chief among these tools is finding out how you manage conflict. If you discover that overall you typically hold out for what you want or conversely always let the other person "win" the argument, you might want to learn how to collaborate so that your interests AND the interests of the other are fulfilled. This is the sweet spot where conflict can be a game changer and spur innovative thinking and cement connection between the people on teams. Simply put, when you and your colleague have gone through the mud together, you come out much stronger.

ACTIVITY!

Take a few minutes to consider how you communicate at work. Don't overthink your answers.

This is not a scientific tool, but it gives you a baseline to help you reflect on your current usage of Authentic Communication.

Authentic Communication Assessment

SCALE OF: 1 (NEVER) **3** (SOMETIMES) **5** (ALWAYS)

1. In meetings, I stay on topic no matter what. _____

2. I refrain from crafting my response while the other person is speaking. _____

3. I have gotten feedback from coworkers that I am a good listener. _____

4. I learn from and about others by hearing what they have to say. _____

5. When dealing with someone who is inauthentic, I speak less and listen more. _____

6. I align my actions with my words. _____

7. I spend time making sure that I back up what I say with evidence. _____

8. I rarely if ever interrupt others during meetings. _____

9. I wait until the information is clear before I make a decision. _____

10. I believe that "cooler heads prevail." _____

11. I check in with my (partner/friends/co-workers) as a sounding board for reality checks on how things are going. _____

12. I make a point of taking the psychological temperature of the room before and after meetings. _____

13. I do unto others as they want done unto them. _____

14. I prefer to speak face to face when it comes to difficult conversations. _____

15. I'm mindful of how much and what I contribute in a conversation. _____

16. I adjust my behavior based on what the other person is feeling. _____

17. I find it helpful to put myself in the shoes of my friends and my frenemies. _____

18. When I run a meeting, I work with the participants to create norms for conduct and process. _____

19. I adhere to established norms of behavior when it comes to meetings and overall communication. _____

20. I constructively assert myself when I disagree with a policy instead of bottling it. _____

21. I am able to freely brainstorm ideas. _____

22. I rarely if ever talk about people behind their back in a destructive way. _____

23. I say positive things about people in my organization behind their backs. _____

24. I find out about and share the stories of times when my team did great work. _____

25. I can hold others accountable without seeming judgmental. _____

26. When I lead a meeting, I work to ensure that all participants have equal air time. _____

27. I work to create bi-directional conversations with people at all levels in my organization. _____

28. I influence others by tailoring my argument in the terms and values that resonant with that particular friend or foe. _____

29. I'm aware of my predisposition to managing differences (avoid, accommodate, compete, compromise or collaborate). _____

30. I'm agile in adopting the conflict style which will optimally enhance my outcome. _____

SCORING

120-150: My Authentic Communication is through the roof.

90-119: My Authentic Communication needs some attention.

30-89: My Authentic Communication needs to go to the emergency room.

My total score

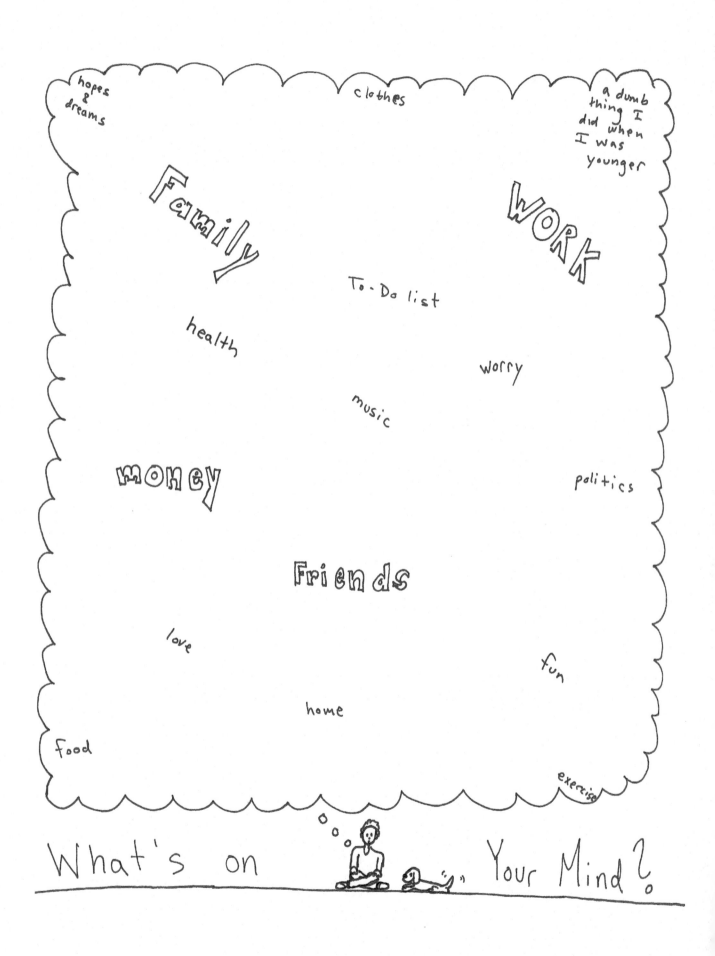

Mindful Communication

IF EVER THERE WAS A TIME to learn how to focus, it's now. We're inundated with information. The daily *New York Times* has more information than the average 17th century nobleman would have been exposed to in a lifetime. We are reminded to stay informed and connected, every minute of every day. In one study by the University of London, subjects who were interrupted while doing office tasks by the dinging and ringing of their phones, even though they were not allowed to answer the messages, were so distracted, their IQ was negatively impacted. In fact, a dinging phone was more disruptive and had a worse negative impact than losing a whole night's sleep or even using marijuana. The short of it is, the constant distraction wipes us out. It makes us dumb and tired.

Ellen Langer, noted Harvard psychologist says that years of research show unequivocally that being present restores "our creativity, psychological well-being and physical health." Among her litany of benefits: improved memory, attention, learning and productivity. Not to mention higher self-esteem, weight loss, innovation and charisma to name a few more.

My brother, Paul, talked about how in high school, playing basketball, he would slip into this state of just being, where nothing else mattered. He said it's almost trancelike. His ability to do this proved helpful years later when he played pool and was able to stay present and not fret over past missed shots or how good a particular opponent was supposed to be. He said pool players call it "deadstroke"…when you're in the zone and focused and can't miss. Hopefully you all can think of times when you have been absolutely absorbed in an activity and how unbelievably good that feels. You aren't thinking about what

1: THE PARKING LOT

2: CONGRUENCE

3: THE PAUSE PRACTICE

4: MINDFUL LISTENING

5: AUTHENTIC SELF-COMMUNICATION

ACTIVITY!

Think about the circumstances when you are most present as you go through the following prompts.

I am most present when I:

I am least present when I:

I've noticed when I do this, I am able to pay more attention:

you're going to be doing the next day or even how well you are performing the task at hand. You are in the moment.

While not exactly extolled on ESPN, mindfulness training is often part of professional sports training. In Gelles' book, *Mindful Work,* he gives example after example of how coaches use mindfulness practices to help players focus. We don't need to be world class athletes to benefit from focus. Gelles writes about a 2010 paper published by Harvard professor David Gilbert called, "A Wandering Mind is an Unhappy Mind." Using an app, participants in the study (more than 5,000 people from 83 countries) were asked throughout the day how they were feeling right at that moment. Results revealed something very interesting. "When people were daydreaming about a delightful fantasy, they were unhappier than when they were focused on the present moment." The best predictor of happiness in this study was if the participants were focused on what they were presently doing. What we do know is when we are fully engaged in our work or a relationship, we feel happier. We feel centered. We aren't stressed or worried about time or what other people think. It's freedom. Being mindful isn't just doing yoga or meditating on a hill at sunrise. Although that can be very nice. But being mindful can happen in our offices, in our kitchens, in our cars, in our everyday. Where is your attention?

THE PARKING LOT ACTIVITY!

Color the picture below of the workers using the Parking Lot.

1. THE PARKING LOT

"...I must stay on track to keep my purpose."
-ALICE WALKER

Have you ever been to a meeting that went long because you and the other members got side-tracked by topics NOT on the agenda? If there is a degree of psychological safety in your group, you are likely to be a victim of this since members feel comfortable sharing ideas and giving insight. That in itself is a wonderful thing and a key ingredient to high performing teams. However, constantly going off topic and going over time can be frustrating.

Sharing ideas and insights can be great, but constantly going off topic and going over time can be frustrating.

So how can we maintain psychological safety and innovative thinking while staying focused and respecting people's time? By using a simple mindful practice called **The Parking Lot.**

Label a whiteboard or a flipchart page and designate a Parking Lot "attendant." Any topic or issue not on the agenda can go on the Parking Lot to be discussed later. This way, the ideas can flow but time and schedules are respected and the meeting stays focused.

Remember, the Parking Lot is not a garbage can. Be sure to get the items in the Parking Lot delegated to the appropriate staff for execution. Some items in the Parking Lot may be useful items in the agenda for future meetings.

WORKSHOP THE PARKING LOT:

How will the Parking Lot enhance the focus and results of my team?

Here's a list of three meetings I lead or participate in that would benefit from the Parking Lot.

1.

2.

3.

How will I introduce and sustain this practice within these sessions?

What obstacles do I foresee in managing the Parking Lot?

Who might be an effective Parking Lot attendant during a meeting
(not the person facilitating the meeting)?

2. CONGRUENCE

"I have long since come to believe that people never mean half of what they say, and that it is best to disregard their talk and judge only their actions."

–DOROTHY DAY

Every day, often several times a day, I watch the anguished face of someone as they tell me that they once *truly* believed in their leader/teammate. They share that ONCE, they would have scaled mountains for them. But that was all before their workplace-heart was broken by the insidious destroyer of teams and dreams: **incongruence.**

Congruence is the act of being aligned, inside and out. Your values are reflected in your words. Your words are reflected in your behaviors. You live your values consistently and authentically. We trust people who are congruent because they do what they say they are going to do. They follow

through which makes us feel that they have integrity. We want to work for congruent leaders. We want to help congruent teammates and flourish on congruent teams. We want to marry congruent partners. We'd like to vote for congruent politicians, too.

Consider how your workplace would be different if everyone adopted the practice of congruence. Congruence is one of many Authentic Communication practices which builds a culture of psychological safety, innovation and high performance. In an optimally congruent workplace, promises are fulfilled (without threats, cajoling or guilt!), employee engagement is healthy, communication is trusted and expectations are clear, which all leaves more time, money and political capital to expend on other interesting and even profitable activities.

> **DEFINITION:**
> **Congruence** is the act of being aligned, inside and out.

How Can I Become Congruent?
How Can My Team Embrace Congruence?

❶ Being congruent requires **self-awareness** to understand your values, interests, principles, goals and yes, even feelings. Journaling, mindfulness, emotional intelligence development, and creating your own personal core values are good places to start. Congruent people are keenly aware of their purpose. Become curious about yourself and take note of what you learn.

❷ Congruence requires healthy levels of **assertiveness and emotional expression** in order to convey interests in a constructive manner. Learn your own preferred style of managing conflict later on in chapter 19.

CONGRUENCE ACTIVITY!

Color the picture below illustrating the concept of **Congruence.**

❸ Congruence requires **self-discipline**, too, as we must resist the urge to play fast and loose with the truth. Congruence also requires you to stay true to your word and follow through on promises. When you encounter that high school frenemy at the grocery store, tap the brakes before you blurt out, "Yes, it's so great seeing you! Let's get lunch!" The power of the Positive No can help you find the right words.

❹ Ask for kind-hearted accountability partners. When you fall out of alignment, you will get the much-needed tap on the shoulder or elbow in the ribs to let you know that you are human. Then, sincerely *feel* sorry, authentically say that you are sorry and intentionally change your *behavior* accordingly (which is all, congruent! Congratulations!).

WORKSHOP CONGRUENCE:

What beliefs are most important to me?

Dorothy Day said she stopped believing what people said and instead looked at what they did to know what they really believed. What actions align with what I believe?

What actions might misalign with what I believe?

What steps can I take to be more congruent?

What beliefs are most important for my team?

How do our words and actions align with our beliefs?

How can my team collectively take steps to be more aligned with what we believe?

THE PAUSE PRACTICE ACTIVITY!

Color the picture below illustrating the concept
of **the Pause Practice.**

3. THE PAUSE PRACTICE

"The two most powerful warriors are patience and time."
-LEO TOLSTOY

"Adopt the pace of nature: her secret is patience."
-RALPH WALDO EMERSON
–DOROTHY DAY

When my family gets together over the holidays, for some of us, interrupting one another is like a competitive sport. The ultimate goal seems to be to talk over one another. It can be loud and raucous. One of the many problems though is we don't listen fully to the other person with whom we're communicating. We're losing about half if not more of the information, and the substance as well as the emotional, relational content of the communication.

Using the Pause Practice would mean waiting for my brother to finish his story before I even think of how I want to respond.

This pause may feel awkward at first because of the new delay between when the speaker finishes and your response. It's helpful to clue in your family or others on your team that you're using the Pause Practice. Most likely, they will think it's respectful and appreciate the fact that you listen the entire way through the conversation.

The Pause Practice can be used electronically as well.

If you've ever gotten an email that felt a little bit hostile, you can imagine how helpful taking time to breathe and formulate a calm response is for everyone involved.

Instead of firing off an angry response, take a pause. Spend time being reflective, seeking to understand before pulling the trigger and firing back a response that you might later regret. The Pause Practice is almost always highly effective in de-escalating hostile situations.

DEFINITION

"relational context of a message"

It's the underlying meaning of a message, the connotation. For example, you might ask your colleague how she's doing and she puts on a smile and says tightly, "Oh, I'm great." You recognize that the relational meaning of "I'm great" is actually, "I'm terrible."

New message   — ⤢ ✕

To Sarah Colantonio

Subject

I wanted to let you know that I don't appreciate how you always monopolize discussion at our weekly meetings. I have a lot of projects, and I really need time to get my work discussed as well. So far, thanks to you, I haven't been able to do that. Can you make sure you make time for me next week?

Thanks.
Kedren

WORK
WISDOM

Send   A 🔗   ▼ ⋮

WORKSHOP THE PAUSE PRACTICE:

A time when I did not pause and regretted my response was:

A time when it benefited me to pause before jumping to a conclusion or decision:

What would have been the cost if I hadn't paused?

I am sometimes impulsive in the following situations:

4. MINDFUL LISTENING

"If there is any hope for us, it lies in... reclaiming ourselves as a listening species."

-MARIA POPOVA (CREATOR OF BRAIN PICKINGS)

President Roosevelt was in the receiving line at the White House one evening and, as a joke, shook the hands of visitors and said smiling, "Welcome to the White House, I killed my grandmother this morning." The visitors nodded, shook his hand, apparently unfazed by the "confession." At last, a visitor took his hand and said with a smirk, "I'm sure she deserved it."

In conference rooms across the country, people are engaged in the high-skilled art of pseudo-listening. We've all done it. Somebody in the front of the room is extolling the meaning behind a graph or client or idea, and we are frowning at them as if listening intently and yet we're in our own world, thinking about our own idea, estimating the time until lunch, or worrying about the next meeting.

What do we miss by not listening? The chance to understand another person. The chance to connect. The ability to be a better decision-maker and problem solver. Research consistently shows that mindful listeners have better interpersonal relationships, tend to get paid more and are promoted more often. Mindful listeners are seen as more likable, more attractive and smarter. Of course they are. Close your eyes and recall the last time someone truly listened to you. Feels fantastic, doesn't it?

Like any practice, meditation, running, yoga, healthy eating, it takes discipline and motivation to become a better listener.

There's a famous listening experiment where some University of Massachusetts students were taught active listening techniques like eye contact, open body posture, asking questions, and generally being engaged when someone else is talking. When a visiting professor came to teach, he spoke in a monotone voice and read from his notes, not connecting with the class at all. One day in class, at a prearranged signal, the students started using these active listening techniques and were gratified to see a change in the professor. He became animated, talking about the material with more excitement. The classroom came alive. It was an experiment though, so again, at another signal, the students stopped using the techniques. The professor tried to get the class back, rather awkwardly but to no avail. Once he realized he couldn't get their attention, he went back to his notes and

MINDFUL LISTENING ACTIVITY!

Color the picture below illustrating the concept of **Mindful Listening**

MINDFUL LISTENING

back to reading in a monotone voice. We imagine that he went home and told his attentive dog, "I was so good today for about 20 minutes. And then I don't know what happened."

If communication was a pie, listening would take up almost half of it. But we aren't really listening. It's a vital and often untapped skill. Do we even know how to listen? I taught public speaking college courses for many years and in those classes, we spent a tiny fraction of the time on the topic of listening. And we certainly did not offer the subject of listening as a separate course.

Kate Murphy, journalist and author of **You're Not Listening** wrote, "Listening is the neglected stepchild of communication research...browse the three-volume, 2,048-page *International Encyclopedia of Interpersonal Communication* and you'll find only one entry specific to listening. And you won't even find *listening* in the index of *The SAGE Handbook of Interpersonal Communication*."

It's surprising that this superpower communication tool gets so little attention. Valerie Martin, in the article, "Listening Is a Verb" says, "It would be astonishing to discover how many problems might be solved if only more of us would seriously and actively listen to those who are trying to communicate to us."

The hard part is acknowledging that we struggle with listening. And harder still is wanting to do something about it. Kevin Sharer, a biotech CEO shares how he started his career in his 30s as the kind of listener focused on "intellectual winning" instead of comprehension. He said his communication was 90% telling and 10% listening. He realized that not only did it need to be closer to 50-50, he also needed a certain amount of humility to listen mindfully. Sharer acknowledges that most of us know that it's important to listen and that it's valuable but that it is often "more lip service than conviction. Listening can be learned but to change your behavior on any important dimension, you've

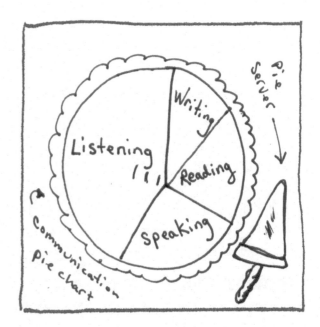

got to have deep self-awareness. You have to change and you have to want to change."

Like any practice: meditation, running, yoga, healthy eating, it takes discipline and motivation to become a better listener. The significant benefits of listening might be motivating to you.

‣ **You are more likable and trustworthy.** In one study of taped conversations, the individuals who spoke less were considered more likable. Not surprisingly, studies also show a positive relationship between listening skills and other social, cognitive and communicative abilities.

‣ **When you listen, you teach the other person to listen as well.** This might take time, but the impact is inevitable.

‣ **You seem smarter.** You will actually be smarter because you'll know more. Studies also show better listeners tend to make more money and have higher positions in organizations.

‣ **You will make fewer mistakes.**

‣ **You will be less stressed and that will make the people around you less stressed.**

THE LISTENING CHALLENGES

To build our listening skills, yes, eye contact, yes, open posture, yes, nodding, yes, clarifying questions. But on a broader scale remember these points. Listening takes work! It is in no way passive.

1. Number one, prepare yourself to listen. Eat breakfast, get a good night's sleep. Mentally and physically, prepare. Listening is an active communication behavior. You're receiving information from someone else, and your brain is doing quite a lot of work to interpret and understand.

2. Secondly, listen between the lines. That means, don't just listen for content. People lie. Or they say things they don't exactly mean or they verbally agree when they don't really agree. Listen for ultimate interests, motivations, emotion—go deep. Look for patterns. Have you noticed that a friend or colleague seems to tell the same story again and again? Look for that. What response are they looking for? How does it serve them to repeat that story? What does it mean for them?

3. Lastly, exercise *appreciative* listening. Notice the people in your life, either in your workplace or at home, who you absolutely love listening to when they speak. What is it about them that makes them so fascinating to you? Try to decipher the skills or traits they exhibit that makes you such a willing audience. Are they good story tellers? Are they passionate? Persuasive? Funny? Eloquent? Once you've figured out what the secret sauce is, look for those things in others. You might be surprised to see that coworker you shy away from actually has a sense of humor. Or that family member has had some fascinating life experience you've never listened long enough to hear about.

Listening is about tapping into your innate curiosity about other people. Celeste Headlee, the radio talk show host, author and TED talk presenter said that curiosity is what makes her such a good interviewer. She is genuinely interested in other people and assumes if she listens long enough, she'll find out some magical, interesting thing about them. And she's never disappointed. Accessing a quality we already have, like curiosity, makes listening sound a lot more fun to practice, doesn't it?

Listening does take practice. The following listening challenges are designed to help concretely hone the ability to absorb, focus, and strengthen those listening muscles. When practiced, be aware that they will impact your relationships in remarkably positive ways. You will become a magnet.

Listening is about tapping into your innate curiosity about other people. Assessing a quality we have, like curiosity, makes listening sound a lot more fun to practice, doesn't it?

Consider adopting one challenge per month or having a friend or partner who will take the challenge on as well.

1. The Lean-in-literally Challenge

Show physical interest and attention to the speaker using eye contact and overall receptive body language.

▶ Consider this survey taken with New York City hospital patients regarding 2-minute visits by doctors. All of the visits were two minutes long, but the doctors who stood to talk to the patients were perceived as spending far less time and not really listening. The doctors who pulled up a chair and sat next to the bed, looking into the patient's eyes, were thought to be truly interested in the patient and spending more time on the visit.

2. The iPhone Challenge

Put it away (physically and emotionally) when you are trying to connect with a fellow human.

▶ One of the greatest gifts you can give another person is your full attention. When I asked my communication class how they felt when they were really listened to, one student said, "I'm surprised." We are so distracted by our dinging notifications. Keep the phone out of sight and focus on the person in front of you.

3. Pregnant Pausing

In other words, The Pause Practice. Let the silence work for you.

▶ In another study with doctors and patients, doctors interrupted patients less than 30 seconds into their description of their problem. If a doctor is meant to diagnose, how is 30 seconds or less going to give them the whole picture? It's not. The study had another iteration where doctors waited to let the patient finish talking. The surprising finding was that on average, patients spoke for only about 90 seconds before stopping but it gave the doctors a far clearer picture of the cause of their patient's illness. On top of that, the doctors who allowed their patients to speak for 90 seconds were perceived to be more likable and competent just by listening. Often our instinct is to jump in with our brilliance and not let other people finish their thought, but we miss out on their core interests and back story if we finish for them.

4. Grow a Third Ear

Listen to hear the other's motivations, anxieties and underlying interests.

▶ This challenge requires the listener to tap into intuition, focus and attention. Theodor Reik, a Freud trained psychoanalyst, wrote a book in 1948 which describes how to understand and relate to others using observation and analysis that requires self-awareness and a deepened awareness of the speaker's interests and motivations. Begin by listening to yourself and then branch out to others. Read between your own lines. Listen for themes. Hear the strength and emphasis of certain words and note sequencing and cadence. You will be surprised at what you learn.

Integrating the practice of listening into your everyday life can transform your relationship with yourself and others. It can lead to greater success in your work and home life. Give it a try. It takes 40 days to start a habit. Why not adopt the practice of mindful listening?

WORKSHOP MINDFUL LISTENING:

I am an exceptional listener when:

There is someone to whom I have trouble listening mindfully. One thing that is interesting about this person is:

Three actions I will take to listen to this person more mindfully are:
1.

2.

3.

The best listener I know is:

My favorite person to listen to is:

They're my favorite person to listen to because:

AUTHENTIC SELF-COMMUNICATION ACTIVITY!

Color the picture below illustrating the concept of **Authentic Self-communication**

5. AUTHENTIC SELF-COMMUNICATION

"Yeah, it's disturbing when someone has no self-awareness."
-MIKE WHITE (SCREENWRITER & ACTOR)

"I think self-awareness is probably the most important thing towards being a champion."
-BILLIE JEAN KING

One of us believes that she is a funny person. She likes to believe that. It's a core belief of hers. Occasionally, though, she'll get feedback that reflects maybe she's not as funny as she thinks she is. In order to maintain her core belief, she will ignore the feedback or the person presenting the feedback because she doesn't like the information that disproves her perception of her own identity.

But seriously, in order to reap the benefits of Authentic Communication in our workplaces, we need everyone to be authentic. Honest. Have high reality testing. Since we can't change other people as much as we would like to, we start with ourselves and ask the question, "Am I telling the truth?"

Cognitive dissonance is the discomfort we feel from holding two or more contradictory beliefs at the same time. Sometimes we're confronted with information that conflicts with our existing beliefs. We become what's called psychologically uncomfortable and we're motivated to try to reduce this dissonance and actively avoid situations and information which increase it. We want to see consistency between our expectations and reality. When we don't have the consistency, we actively work to reduce the dissonance often by ignoring or denying information that conflicts with our beliefs.

In order to get to real maturity and understand the complexities of other humans including ourselves, we have to become more comfortable with the dissonance. With the paradoxes. With the contradictory data. And even examine it.

In *Rising Strong,* Brené Brown talks about arguments with her husband when he's presenting data that is dissonant with her perceived version of herself. She has this very handy phrase that you can use, too. It helps to separate her perception of reality from reality so that she's able to counteract the need to reduce that dissonance. Her response to her husband begins with, "The story I'm starting to tell myself is that...you don't respect me" or "the story I'm starting to tell myself is that you think I'm irresponsible".

In Kedren's case, when she is looking at data that is contradictory to her own identity, she should probably use the phrase "The story I'm starting to tell myself is that you think I'm not funny."

One of the benefits to Authentic Self-Communication and examining our beliefs more closely is that often we have disempowering, unhelpful beliefs that limit our growth and suppress our joy.

DEFINITION
Cognitive dissonance:
The discomfort from holding two or more contradictory beliefs at the same time.

Through examination, we can poke holes in these unhelpful perceptions and live more authentically.

> *Ring the bells that still can ring*
> *Forget your perfect offering*
> *There is a crack, a crack in everything*
> *That's how the light gets in.*

- LEONARD COHEN

Two simple concrete ways to let in the light can be found in Byron Katie's book, *Loving What Is.* **The following four questions are insightful to open your mind to Authentic Self-Communication.**

▶ **BRYON KATIE'S FOUR QUESTIONS**

1 Is it true?

2 Am I absolutely sure it's true?

3 How do I react, what happens when I believe that thought?

4 Who would I be without that thought?

▶ **Another Byron Katie technique is called THE TURNAROUND**

In the Turnaround, imagine a disempowering story you have that is plaguing you. For example, *"My co-worker doesn't respect me."*

1 Take the story and turn it around to the self: *"I don't respect me."* Come up with one or two examples of times when you didn't respect yourself.

2 Next, turn around to the other: *"I don't respect my co-worker."* Often, the light bulb goes off in our heads with this turnaround statement. Find an example or two of times when this statement was evident.

3 Lastly, turn it around to the opposite: *"My co-worker DOES respect me."* And find an example of when this was true.

These techniques help us consider our story from a different perspective, and shake loose from unhelpful beliefs or assumptions.

WORKSHOP AUTHENTIC SELF-COMMUNICATION:

Three core identity traits I believe about myself are:

1.

2.

3

Sometimes I do things that are misaligned with the identity I have constructed of myself. An example:

The following is a disempowering story I tell myself:

Is it true?

Am I absolutely sure it is true?

What happens when I have this belief?

CONTINUES ON NEXT PAGE ▶

WORKSHOP AUTHENTIC SELF-COMMUNICATION (CONTINUED):

THE TURNAROUND
The disempowering belief I've been telling myself is...

Turn around to the self: _____
List three examples of this.

1.

2.

3.

Turn around to the other: _____
List three examples of this.

1.

2.

3.

Turn around to the opposite: _____
List three examples of this.

1.

2.

3.

Emotionally Intelligent Communication

THINK OF THE BEST BOSS you ever had. Now think about what made them the best boss you've ever had. Great bosses are insightful. They care about you. They are incredible communicators. They read the room. They listen. More often than not, the traits we assign to our great bosses are all products of their emotional intelligence.

While cognitive intelligence is important in the workplace and in communication, how we utilize emotional intelligence predicts how successful we'll actually be at work. Interestingly, the author Thomas Stanley wrote about a survey of 733 multi-millionaires who were asked what factors most contributed to their success. The top five were:

▸ Being honest

▸ Being disciplined

▸ Getting along with others

▸ Having a supportive spouse

▸ Working harder than most people

All of those answers connect to emotional intelligence. The great thing is, while IQ is fairly fixed, our EQ (Emotional Intelligence Quotient) is not fixed at all. It's completely changeable.

You might be curious about what exactly emotional intelligence is and how it can help you with communication. Emotional intelligence has four major components: how we perceive and express ourselves, how we build and maintain interpersonal relationships, how we cope with stress, and how we weave emotional data into how we solve a problem or make a decision.

Emotionally Intelligent Communication requires self-awareness, self-regulation and the ability to recalibrate how you communicate feelings. The following concrete practices can help you sharpen your Emotional Intelligence and deepen the exchanges you have with others: Check-ins, Check-outs; The Platinum Rule; Self-Regulation; Richness of Mediums; and Empathy.

6: CHECK-INS, CHECK-OUTS

7: THE PLATINUM RULE

8: SELF-REGULATION

9: RICHNESS OF MEDIUMS

10: EMPATHY

CHECK-INS AND CHECK-OUTS ACTIVITY!

Color the picture below of the team members using the one-word Check-ins and Check-outs.

6. CHECK-INS AND CHECK-OUTS

"Who questions much, shall learn much, and retain much."

— FRANCIS BACON

After a particularly intense meeting, I felt drained. The group we were facilitating had just gone through a hard discussion and I was worried they would be leaving our office angry. Kedren closed the session with a question. "Let's go around the room and say one word that describes how you are feeling about the new behaviors we're going to adopt going forward." I winced. This was going to be bloody. I was particularly worried about the gentleman sitting next to me. He had seemed to be scowling for the majority of the meeting. What happened next was fascinating. When it was his turn to speak, he paused for a moment and then said softly, "I'm inspired. Encouraged. Oh yeah, only one word." He smiled shyly. I was blown away. I had no idea how the meeting had actually gone for him. I was so busy worrying about the vulnerable conversation they had been having, I missed how meaningful it was for this team.

DEFINITION
One-word-check-in and
One-word-check-out:
An emotionally intelligent question that allows us to take the temperature of the team before or after a meeting.

The Check-In or Check-Out is an emotionally intelligent question that allows us to take the temperature of the team before or after a meeting. Check-ins and Check-outs are conducted as a round robin (going around the circle) so that every member of the team has a chance to participate. If the Check-in question is framed well, you can discern the energy levels and optimism at the meeting. The meeting facilitator begins by asking the participants to share one word (hyphens are used liberally here!) that is a truthful answer to the question framed by the facilitator. Often, questions are along the lines of, "Describe how you're feeling about the strategy we're discussing today" or "Share one word that describes what strength you plan to bring to this effort today." One of the greatest benefits of the Check-in is that it breaks the psychological ice. When everyone on the team has already spoken in a meeting, it is so much easier to speak up a second time.

As Kedren did in the above example, you can take the pulse at the conclusion of the meeting with a Check-out. One goal of a thoughtful Check-out question is to extract the most desired outcome from the meeting. A One-word-check-out question might be, "Share one word that describes your most important takeaway from this meeting" or "What is one word that describes the most critical next step?" By creating a team norm of Check-in or Check-outs, people come to expect and optimally use this tool for the energy of the group and the benefit of the meeting outcome.

WORKSHOP CHECK-INS AND CHECK-OUTS:

Here are three ways I can "take the temperature" of the people in a meeting before I dive into the content.

1.

2.

3.

I can use this information to enhance the outcome of the meeting in this way:

I can use this information to enhance the cohesion of my team in this way:

A helpful "check-in" question to ask at the next meeting I am leading:

A helpful "check-out" question to ask at the next meeting I will be leading:

THE PLATINUM RULE ACTIVITY!

Color the picture below illustrating a violation of the Platinum Rule.

7. THE PLATINUM RULE

"Do not do unto others as you would that they should do unto you.
Their tastes may be different."

— GEORGE BERNARD SHAW

In a giant hotel conference room with over 200 people gathered to hear a popular mindfulness guru speak, I nervously listened to the instructions for an exercise. *"Find someone you don't know, stand face to face and ask them, what do you want? Continue to ask them until we let you know when it is time to switch. Go."*

I didn't know one person at the conference so I didn't think it would be difficult to find a stranger, but alas, everyone around me was pairing up so quickly, I was without a partner. Finally, a late comer dashed in and was paired up with me. I was relieved. She looked kind.

As we started the exercise, I was amazed by how quickly we connected. *"What is it that you want?"* The repetition in questioning helped us go beyond surface answers. It gave us permission to explore within ourselves, *"What do I really want?"*

We all have heard of the Golden Rule and it is helpful. But imagine this, if you will. Do you drink coffee? If you do, do you have a particular way you like it? I do. I like a good bit of vanilla almond milk creamer in my coffee. Maybe you prefer iced coffee or you like it black, or just with sugar. Let's imagine that every day I come into work and bring you a coffee the way I take it. How long until you say, *"Sarah, please stop. The way you drink coffee is disgusting!"* Sure, I thought I was being nice, but I was imposing my coffee preferences onto you.

The Platinum Rule posits that you do to others as they would want done to them. If I had used the Platinum Rule, I would have said, *"Hey, I want to bring you coffee tomorrow. How do you like it?"* and that would have made us both happy.

In order to collaborate or create mutually satisfying solutions to problems, you must become adept at the practice of asking, *"What do you want?"* and also, *"Why?"*

ACTIVITY

Ask your colleague or your partner if they have a few minutes to conduct the following exercise:

Face each other.

Look at each other.

Person A asks Person B, "What do you want?"

Person B answers whatever comes to their mind.

Person A repeats the question.

Do this 5 times.

Then reverse roles. Have Person B ask Person A, "What do you want?"

The What-Do-You-Want Exercise

Instructions: Ask your colleague or partner if they have a few minutes to conduct the following exercise.

1. Face eachother.
2. Ask the other, "What do you want?"
3. Let them answer with whatever comes to mind.
4. Repeat the question.
5. Let them answer.
6. Do this 5x.
7. Switch roles. Let them ask you, and you get to answer.

P.S. it gets less awkward, I promise.

WORKSHOP THE PLATINUM RULE:

CIRCLE ONE: When I completed the "What do you want" activity, I knew what I wanted.

TRUE   FALSE

I said I wanted:

1.

2.

3.

4.

5.

CIRCLE ONE: It was   **EASY   HARD   GOT EASIER**   to say what I wanted.

CIRCLE ONE: It was   **EASY   HARD   GOT EASIER**   to listen to what the other person wanted.

They said:

1.

2.

3.

4.

5.

SELF-REGULATION ACTIVITY!

Color the picture below of the concept of self-regulation.

8. SELF-REGULATION

"Elegance is refusal."

— COCO CHANEL

"Breviloquence: (noun); Speaking briefly and concisely

— WORDSMITH.ORG

Imagine you are 4 years old and have agreed to play a game with an adult. The adult sets a marshmallow on the table and lets you know they have to run out for 15 minutes and if you want, you can have the treat but if you wait until they get back, you can have two marshmallows. Two! What would you do? Did we mention the room has only a chair, the table the marshmallow sits atop and the marshmallow. That's it.

In this famous experiment, the researcher, Walter Mischel was not only interested in the display of self-control, a surprising 2/3 of the kids held out, by the way, but years later he went back to the participants and checked in on them. Some fascinating results were found. Of the kids who ate the one marshmallow right away, they as young adults demonstrated impulsive, stubborn and indecisive behavior. Of the children who did not succumb to temptation, they incredibly had better social skills, exhibited better coping skills, and demonstrated concretely in grades and SAT scores, were much better students.

DEFINITION
Self-regulation:
The ability to monitor and control our own behaviors, emotions and thoughts in accordance with a particular situation.

If you really want to demonstrate respect for your co-workers, Self-regulate. We all know people who don't have a filter. But Self-regulation is the ability to monitor and control our own behaviors, emotions and thoughts in accordance with a particular situation. It involves filtering and modulating behavior.

The ability to Self-regulate is not only a skill correlated with cognitive intelligence, but it's a skill that can be honed and is a huge part of emotional intelligence. A good example of Self-Regulation in communication might be utilizing the One-Word-Check-In or Check-Out during meetings. It's concise, it's honest and it's an effective way for the team to know what's on your mind.

In contrast, dysregulation is what happens when there's a mismatch between the goals, responses, and modes of expression. For example, if you used the Check-In to pontificate and take over "the floor."

In order to achieve optimal team outcomes, ideally, we as individuals and those on our teams will practice Self-regulation in our communications. Regulating our communication is a collective duty which reaps exceptional collective benefits. Self-regulation honors those with whom you are communicating because it respects their time and recognizes their ability to absorb only so much information. By polishing your thoughts in line with goals and values, prior to speaking, you have given a gift to the listener. Because of your judicious use of the shared air space, listeners will want to spend time with you in the future because they have experienced this meaningful, behavioral respect that you've demonstrated to them through Self-regulated communication.

We worked with a team that had an impressive Self-Regulation practice. They were a marketing team and while much of their communication was face to face, they also emailed each other A LOT. They had a rule as a team that emails could be 5 sentences. Of course their ingenious workaround was it could and probably would have attachments, but it forced them to be concise and to the point in their electronic communication. Self-regulation requires clarity around long-term interests and the values of the team members so we might want to alter the amount or the volume of communication we share considering the long-term interests and values of our team. We may regulate the tone or the types of information we share. We may want to have 5 sentence emails. Can you imagine?!

Real authenticity requires major self-monitoring. We can begin Self-regulating by considering the long view, knowing our teams' values and gaining real deep knowledge about our own individual and collective emotional intelligence. Self-regulation will look different across teams. But naming and honoring the importance of Self-regulation is essential to building psychologically safe, emotionally intelligent workplaces.

WORKSHOP
SELF-REGULATION:

Self-regulation entails filtering and consciously choosing what we communicate and with whom. Has a leader/teammate or partner ever suggested I alter the volume or content of what I communicate? What have I been told?

How can I modulate my communication in order to enhance the results of my relationships, while still being authentic and assertive?

9. RICHNESS OF MEDIUMS

"I can't text, ya know, I'm not charming via text. "

"Well, maybe you should stop texting."

"It's not just texting, it's email, it's voicemail, it's snail mail."

"That's regular mail."

"Whatever, none of it's working. I had this guy leave me a voicemail at work so I called him at home and then he emailed my blackberry and so I texted to his cell and then he emailed me to my home account and the whole thing just got out of control and I miss the days when you have one phone number, and one answering machine and that one answering machine housed one cassette tape and that one cassette tape either had a message from the guy or it didn't. Now I have to go around checking all these different portals just to get rejected by seven different technologies. It's exhausting."

— DREW BARRYMORE, THE 2009 FILM *HE'S JUST NOT THAT INTO YOU*

In the book *Perfect Pitch*, advertiser John Steel talks about the time his team was going to pitch Steve Jobs back in 1997. While waiting for Jobs to show up, two guys from Apple's marketing department bombarded the advertising team with an hour and a half, Death By Powerpoint, "agency briefing." Steel said, "Our presenter seemed oblivious to our pain; in the half light, he brought up slide after slide, graph after graph, table after table, each densely packed with numbers and with commentary he read verbatim." Not only is that boring, but it is the least rich medium to convey information.

Richness has to do with the amount of information a medium can carry. It depends on the availability of feedback, the use of multiple cues, the use of effective language, and the extent to which the communication has a personal focus. Face to face verbal communication is the richest medium. You use many cues, including voice, tone, facial expressions, and body language during a face to face interaction. Plus, with face to face, you can more easily create a personal focus to your message.

Just when Steel and his colleagues thought they were going to pass out from boredom, Jobs came in, and got down to business. He turned off the projector, took a marker and drew over a dozen boxes on the dry erase board, then crossed out all but two. He explained that those two boxes represented the two projects he wanted Apple to work on (one was the iMac). Then he explained what he wanted from the ad agency and what

RICHNESS OF MEDIUMS ACTIVITY!

Color the picture below of the richness of mediums.

message he wanted to craft for Apple users. Steel writes, "He had explained his strategy for the company in a little less than five minutes and he told us how he saw the role of communications in not much more than 60 seconds. The only visual aids he used were produced live using a marker and a dry erase board. Yet they seemed as vivid as any expensively produced slides or videos we've ever seen."

The impact Jobs had on that group of ad executives came through in how he engaged with them in an immediate way. He didn't need to rely on (ironically enough) technology, but on his presence. It behooves us to consider our medium in our communication.

You'll notice that the top four richest mediums are bi-directional in nature, when you are giving *and* receiving communication. Even if you are devoted to hand-written notecards and illustrated postcards, alas, that text message is still richer (but maybe not as artful or meaningful).

What will be the most effective? Here's the ranking of communication mediums from the richest to the least rich:

1. Face-to-face in person
2. Synchronous Virtual FaceTime, Zoom, Teams, Slack, Google Hangouts, with camera on
3. Phone with no camera
4. Electronic messaging like e-mail or text
5. Personal written letters, notes or memos
6. Formal written reports or documents
7. Formal data analysis like graphs or statistical reports

WORKSHOP RICHNESS OF MEDIUMS:

What is the communication medium I prefer the most when managing a difficult situation? Why?

A time when this medium was really beneficial:

A time when this preferred medium cost me:

A medium I want to try to use more:

Because of the increase in remote work, face to face communication became less frequent. In order to compensate, I increased the usage of the following mediums:

MATCH THE MEDIUM WITH HOW YOU INTEND TO COMMUNICATE DURING FUTURE SITUATIONS LIKE THIS.

▶ My partner is consistently ignoring my texts.

▶ My boss emailed and said they need to talk to me.

▶ A colleague on the other coast is experiencing signs of burnout.

▶ My best friend's partner just broke up with them.

▶ My employee is doing a bad job.

▶ My boss gave me a poor review on a project I thought was fantastic.

▶ My grandmother sent me a sweater.

▶ My boss' boss wants to hear about the progress of my team's big project.

▶ I want to schedule dinner with a busy friend.

▶ A remote worker is increasingly missing deadlines.

▶ An internal project needs to be organized to gain momentum from the team.

O FACETIME CALL

O TEXT

O FACE TO FACE IN AN OFFICE

O PHONE CALL

O PRESENTATION

O HANDWRITTEN NOTE

O EMAIL

O WRITTEN REPORT

O FACE TO FACE OVER COFFEE

O ZOOM MEETING

O SLACK/TEAMS

10. EMPATHY

"I think we all have empathy. We may not have enough courage to display it."
— MAYA ANGELOU

*"When you show deep empathy towards others, their defensive
energy goes down, and positive energy replaces it."*
— STEPHEN COVEY

Empathy is not just the ability to feel another's feelings but also the ability to recalibrate our behaviors based on the other person's feelings. Empathy is a critical dimension of emotionally intelligent communication because it allows us to quickly connect with another person by establishing our shared humanity in our difficulties. Our own imperfection and woundedness allows us to put ourselves on the same team, in the same boat and in the struggle with the person across from us. Empathy enables seemingly opposing parties to focus on creating mutually beneficial solutions.

Empathy plays a significant role in Emotional Labor which requires us to regulate our emotions as part of our job duties. Our emotions become commodities. In the 1999 comedy "Office Space," Jennifer Aniston's waitress character gets in trouble for not having enough "flair" on her uniform for work. To be a successful server at Chotchkie's, she

was expected to radiate enthusiasm and fun at all times while on the clock. That took a toll and she eventually quit the job.

In the world of Emotional Labor, the difference between Surface Acting and Deep Acting is key. Surface Acting looks like pretending to be enthusiastic and/or suppressing emotions (aka, "shining it on"). But Deep Acting is a process where employees exhibit their internal feelings which are aligned with organizational expectations. Not surprisingly, Deep Acting produces greater employee engagement and organizational well-being than Surface Acting. We work with a local organization that does meaningful work to help refugees. Despite frustration over legislation blocking their efforts, the people in that

Empathy also de-escalates conflict and opens new boundaries and collaborative contacts where there might be a lack of trust or perceived threat.

EMPATHY ACTIVITY!

Color the picture below of Empathy and Deep Perspective-taking.

Mindful Listening

Look for the human behind every thing

Empathy

Be curious about strangers

organization are bonded by their shared mission. Instead of burning out, they are experiencing renewed resolve to help the people they are committed to serving.

Deep Acting is greatly enhanced and accelerated by taking the perspective of the client, customer, student or patient. Perspective-taking and empathy require understanding the situation from the other person's point of view. Empathy reduces feelings of anger towards the other. Research has repeatedly demonstrated that while surface acting causes emotional exhaustion on the job, empathy and deep acting create positive results for the employee and, for example, in the healthcare field, better quality of care for patients and enhanced mental health for physicians. Empathy also de-escalates conflict and opens new boundaries and collaborative contacts where there might be a lack of trust or perceived threat.

There are also three concrete tools that can help you become more empathetic.

❶ The first tool is **mindful listening.** Remember that you are not just listening to what's being said but also what's NOT being said.

❷ The second technique is **"looking for the human behind every thing."** For example, when you have your coffee in the morning, think about that person who picked those beans. What's her morning like? Or as you button your shirt, think about the person who sewed on those buttons. Being curious about the people behind the object strengthens our empathy muscles.

❸ A third concrete tool for boosting your empathy is to be **curious about strangers.** You can even interact with them. Talk to them about their lives, their kids, their joys and you will feel how closely connected we are.

EMPATHY ACTIVITY!

We can learn to empathize in our behavior and our communication. To get a baseline of your current ability, you can take the empathy assessment by neuropsychologist, Simon Baron Cohen called "Reading the Mind in the Eyes." Go online and search the *New York Times'* October 3, 2013 article **"Can You Read People's Emotions"** and take the assessment.

WORKSHOP EMPATHY:

How can I incorporate empathy into my workplace interactions?

Here are three ways I can foster my own empathy to improve communication in my professional life.

1.

2.

3.

I remember a time when a colleague expressed empathy and it deepened our relationship:

When others are empathetic toward me, I feel:

There are a couple of things that make it difficult for me to put myself in the shoes of another person.

1.

2.

Go online and search for Brené Brown's animated short video on Empathy. How does Brown distinguish between empathy and sympathy?

I will adopt two new empathetic behaviors including:

1.

2.

Psychologically Safe Communication

AS THE STORY GOES in ancient Greek mythology, Cassandra was blessed with the gift of seeing the future but frustrated with the curse that no one would ever believe her. Today, a Cassandra culture in the workplace is one that lacks psychological safety. Imagine being a nurse and the doctor you are working with has prescribed what you think is perhaps too high of a dose to a patient. However, last month when you noticed something potentially amiss and you brought it up to the doctor, he leveled you, telling you to stay in your lane and not question his orders.

The Harvard researcher, Dr. Amy Edmondson, did not set out to discover the phenomenon of Psychological Safety. In fact, in her book, *Fearless Organizations,* she writes that her initial research was to hypothesize, "the most effective teams would make the fewest errors." When she looked at the data, it appeared the variance showed something altogether different. It appeared that the more effective teams were the ones who "apparently make more, not fewer, mistakes than the less strong teams." And not just a little bit. It was a statistically significant correlation. At first, she was worried about the findings. Then she had a revelation. "What if the better teams had a climate of openness that made it easier to report and discuss errors? The good teams, don't *make* more mistakes, they *report* more." When she examined the data further, she found it was true.

Edmondson defines Psychological Safety as the feeling that at work, you can take interpersonal

11: GROUND RULES

12: ROUGH DRAFT

13: THE SPEAK-NOW-OR-FOREVER-HOLD-YOUR PEACE RULE

14: NON-TRIANGULATION/DIRECT NEGOTIATION

15: APPRECIATIVE COMMUNICATION

DEFINITION
Psychologically Safe Communication (according to Dr. Amy Edmondson):
The feeling that at work, you can take interpersonal risks, you can make a mistake, speak up, and there is enough respect and trust among your co-workers that you can be honest and open.

risks, you can make a mistake, speak up, and there is enough respect and trust among your co-workers that you can be honest and open. Reimagine the nurse/doctor scenario in a Psychologically Safe environment. The nurse warns the doctor and the doctor appreciates the intervention. Or even if the nurse wasn't correct, the doctor was still open to the feedback and treated the exchange as a teachable moment. As Edmondson notes in her book, fear reduces our ability to learn. But in a Psychologically Safe environment, learning thrives.

Lack of Psychological Safety can be a disaster. Edmondson cites the well-known cases of Volkswagon and Wells Fargo. "[It] was not the result of one bad apple but a system that demanded hitting targets so ambitious they could only be met by deceit...managers sent a clear message: produce-or else."

You might not be experiencing those kinds of extreme cases, but you might relate to a) not wanting to speak up because you don't want to look foolish, b) assuming that the person in charge knows better, c) finding it easier to be quiet and d) thinking that "Nobody will listen to me anyway." But the problem with all of these scenarios, Edmondson says, is that the team misses out on the diverse perspectives which causes mediocrity

and untapped collective genius. It's "the innovation that didn't happen" and it's almost always invisible.

I recall in a meeting, a colleague said, "I'm sure everyone has thought of this already, but..." and we hadn't! Thankfully, she spoke up! In a Psychologically Safe workplace, everyone is reminded that their perspective is necessary for success. Diversity of perspectives makes us smarter, more innovative and more creative.

Okay, great, but how?
Edmondson lays it out:

SET THE STAGE: A COO of a children's hospital had a goal of "100% patient safety for the hospitalized children under her care." In order to set the stage for Psychological Safety, she helped create a "shift in perspective [that] would prove essential to helping people feel safe speaking up about problems, mistakes and risks they saw."

INVITE PARTICIPATION: Create structures that make participation easier. Being curious and inviting feedback helps people in the organization be open to give their input. Instead of asking "did you see lots of mistakes or harm?" that same COO would ask staff, "Was everything as safe as you would like it to have been this week for your patients?"

RESPOND PRODUCTIVELY: If I invite you to participate and then belittle your idea, I've squandered the Psychological Safety that might have been achieved. Be open and appreciative of the feedback. Reinforce the importance of the feedback.

As Edmondson says, "When a leader reminds people that the context in which we work is full of uncertainty—that is, it is complex and profoundly interdependent—they're creating a logical case for the fact that voice is needed. No one knows all the answers, and everyone could have a crucial piece of the puzzle."

The research is clear. Teams that have psychological safety are able to achieve better outcomes because they aren't afraid to joke around, be vulnerable, make mistakes, and take greater risks. Creativity and innovation can flourish. The following practices help foster psychological safety in teams. We can't afford to work in psychologically unsafe workplaces. With perpetual change and innovation, having Psychological Safety on our teams will make it more exciting and fun to go to work, but it's also better for scaling positive impact.

Empathy de-escalates conflict and opens new boundaries and collaborative contacts where there might be a lack of trust or perceived threat.

GROUND RULES ACTIVITY!

Color the picture below of Ground Rules.

11. GROUND RULES

"If you paint in your mind a picture of bright and happy expectations, you put yourself into a condition conducive to your goal."

— NORMAN VINCENT PEALE

The boardroom is packed. Your slide deck is blazing on the big screen. You're doing it, you're presenting your big idea to the decision makers in the company. And then you notice, right in front of you, the CEO is checking his phone. Your heart sinks. Your confidence wavers. A quick scan of the room and you notice he's not the only one. There's an associate over there who has her phone under the table but it's obvious what she's doing. And your supposed friend is peeking at his phone, too. What do you do? If you could turn back time, you could have created Ground Rules.

Ground Rules create a set of clear, expected behaviors setting the norms for a team or even during a meeting. Ground Rules are typically established with input from all of the participants at the beginning of the meeting or during the forming of a team. The facilitator explains the goal of the Ground Rules first, which may be to create a safe environment, to keep focus on the agenda, to facilitate ideation and possibly come to a decision. Team members are asked to share concrete suggestions for behaviors that will enhance the outcomes of the group. They may be written or typed onto a chalkboard, whiteboard, screen or flipchart and all of the members of the group consider and digest the list. Once the list is created, the facilitator asks all the team members if they are comfortable with adopting the rules. If not, you can edit until the group is satisfied. Once accepted, the facilitator asks everyone to commit to the Ground Rules. An enforcer, someone other than the leader can be selected to enforce the rules so that the leader can focus her attention on the agenda.

Ground Rules should be used to establish the following systems:

▶ For meetings
▶ For dealing for conflict inside and outside the team
▶ For dealing with unmet expectations
▶ For project planning
▶ For communicating with each other

DEFINITION
Ground Rules (according to MIT):
Systems that are used by teams to define the way the team members will work together. Ground Rules also establish boundaries for the team; they specify how the members will act when completing the project. Ground Rules should be clear, specific and not general or ambiguous.

A few examples of Ground Rules:

▶ Everyone is responsible for enforcing Ground Rules.

▶ All meetings will begin and end on time; no session will run longer than 2 hours.

▶ Proceed as long as there is a majority of the team present.

▶ No phone calls—emergency interruptions only.

▶ Minimize or eliminate side conversations.

▶ One person will speak at a time.

▶ While generating ideas, withhold debate and criticism.

▶ Treat everyone's ideas with respect.

▶ Suspend judgment until everyone has been heard.

▶ While disagreeing or debating, focus comments on the facts and not on personalities.

▶ Avoid using acronyms unless known by everyone.

▶ If we reach an impasse, use the "Parking Lot."

▶ Try to reach consensus on key decisions, but don't rush.

▶ Speak from the heart.

▶ Listen to understand, not to respond.

▶ We all must be able to support and defend all major decisions of this group.

▶ Read agenda before attending meeting.

▶ Give advance warning to all parties if you will be absent or late for a meeting.

▶ Be concise, don't waste time in meetings by repeating what has already been said or is irrelevant.

▶ Only one-minute tangents are allowed.

WORKSHOP GROUND RULES:

The most unproductive behavior that occurs during meetings in my workplace is:

I think maybe this behavior persists because:

What would happen if my team stopped that behavior?

3 Ground Rules which would create the norms to prevent this behavior might be:

1.

2.

3.

An upcoming meeting when I can use Ground Rules might be:

Two things I can do to prepare myself and my team to optimally use Ground Rules might be:

1.

2.

ROUGH DRAFT ACTIVITY!

Color the picture below of the team needing the Rough Draft concept.

12. ROUGH DRAFT

At a nearby Buddhist monastery...

"Said a disappointed visitor, 'Why has my stay here yielded no fruit?'"

"Could it be because you lacked the courage to shake the tree?"

— *ONE MINUTE WISDOM*, ANTHONY DE MELLO

A Stanford University psychologist gave a series of puzzles to kids in an elementary school. The first batch was easy and the kids solved them handily. Then she gave them the hard puzzles. A funny thing happened. While some kids were frustrated with the difficult puzzles and gave up, and some lied about why they couldn't do the puzzle ("oh yeah, I have this puzzle at home, I've already done it."), others shocked her. Some of the kids were pumped about the new hard puzzle. They dug in. They liked the challenge. One kid exclaimed, "Yes! I was hoping I would learn something today." Intrigued by these responses, she launched into research that would span years. The researcher, Dr. Carol Dweck wrote a book about all of this called **Mindset: the New Psychology of Success.** She said, "Not only [were these kids} not discouraged by failure, they didn't even think they were failing. They thought they were learning."

Some of us are predisposed to a **Fixed Mindset** and we relate to statements like, "You are a certain kind of person and there is not much that can be done to really change that." This sort of mindset can be paralyzing. If I believe I have to be an artistic genius to draw a cartoon, I'll never sit down to do it. If I have an idea I want to share at work but I don't know exactly if it's viable or how it looks to make it happen, I won't bring it up in the meeting.

Growth Mindset is an ability to take difficulty and find the challenge, the adventure in it. It's a *learning from mistakes* kind of attitude. Looking at obstacles as opportunities. Fortunately, we don't have to be *born* with a Growth Mindset to enjoy the benefits of it. In fact, Dr. Dweck claims she has always had a Fixed Mindset and is grateful she can take measures to remember to have a Growth Mindset about challenges that come her way. Our mindset is changeable. If we can shift our perspective about difficulties being a bad thing all the time, we might be able to grow from it. Achieve something better because of it. Dweck says that people with a Growth Mindset don't just seek challenges, they thrive on it. They want to stretch themselves. She gives the example of superstar soccer player Mia Hamm. She quotes Hamm, "I've been playing up all my life, I've challenged myself with players older, bigger, more skilled,

more experienced-better than me." She played with her older brother, then when she was 10, she played on the 11-year old boys team, then in college, she joined the number one team in the nation.

During a session at a local college, we discovered a device that aids in demonstrating a Growth Mindset while also fostering psychological safety at work. A student offered a simple phrase that worked for her and a former team. Before giving a suggestion that hadn't already been thought through completely, team members would say, *"Rough draft, what if we..."* and float their idea. It's easy and especially helpful too for perfectionists who might normally stay silent. It allows people to loosen up a little. To come up with really creative ideas, we have to get something down. Work it over later. Author Anne Lamott wrote, "Almost all good writing begins with terrible first efforts. You need to start somewhere. Start by getting something, anything, down on paper. What I've learned to do when I sit down to work on a shitty first draft is to quiet the voices in my head." At Work Wisdom, we've gotten to an organizational norm where we advance half-baked ideas all the time. This very workbook was a rough draft idea.

ACTIVITY!

Answer yes or no to the following:

1. Your intelligence is something that you can't change very much.

2. You can learn new things, but you can't really change how intelligent you are.

3. No matter how much intelligence you have, you can always change it quite a bit.

4. You can always substantially change how intelligent you are.

5. You are a certain kind of person and there is not much that can be done to really change that.

6. No matter what kind of person you are, you can always change substantially.

7. You can do things differently, but the important parts of who you are can't really be changed.

8. You can always change basic things about the kind of person you are.

....

KEY: Answering yes to 1, 2, 5, 7 is **Fixed Mindset**

Answering yes to 3, 4, 6, 8 is **Growth Mindset**

WORKSHOP ROUGH DRAFT:

Experiment with Rough Draft.

Areas of my life where I demonstrate a Growth Mindset are:

Areas of my life when I notice I might have more of a Fixed Mindset are:

The idea I have that I've been wanting to present at HOME but haven't is:

I haven't presented the idea because:

The idea I have that I've been wanting to present at WORK but haven't is:

I haven't presented the idea because:

I could utilize Rough Draft in my OFFICE to make it easier to present ideas by :

ACTIVITY!

Color the picture below of co-workers following the Speak-Now-or-Forever-Hold-Your-Peace-Rule.

13. THE SPEAK-NOW-OR-FOREVER-HOLD-YOUR-PEACE RULE

"A lot of people are afraid to say what they want.
That's why they don't get what they want."

— MADONNA

A large haircare and beauty product company was struggling to be productive as a team. Stress was running high because profits were declining and they were in danger of bankruptcy. When decisions were being made, they were being ruminated about for weeks and months long after the fact. This habit of "Monday morning quarterbacking" created ill-will and paranoia among team members. An outside consultant was brought in and was able to pinpoint the problem and suggested they implement the Speak-Now-or-Forever-Hold-Your-Peace. The rule posits that input would be solicited up front, the decision would be made, and that after a certain number of days or weeks, the team would stop picking apart a decision after the fact. After a certain amount of time, the window to give an opinion would close, a decision would be reached and everyone would accept it and move forward.

Speak-Now-Or-Forever-Hold-Your-Peace promotes the creation of solutions before the decision is made, of improvements and of evolution. It helps teams focus on embracing the constructive sequence for input.

Once implemented, the practice brought harmony within the ranks of that beauty care company. Not only did they save money, they were able to rebound and avoid bankruptcy. A Psychologically Safe culture emerged and made a difference in their success.

Adopting the Speak-Now-or-Forever-Hold-Your-Peace rule helps remind people to speak up if they disagree or have different ideas. After a decision has been made, and there's been a bit of time for it to really absorb, everyone can move in the same direction of adoption and execution.

WORKSHOP THE SPEAK-NOW-OR-FOREVER-HOLD-YOUR-PEACE RULE:

A time when my team made a decision to move forward with a new plan, policy or venture and there was full commitment from the team:

A time when there was not collective support of a new initiative but rather dissension that continued long after the policy was adopted and implemented:

14. NON-TRIANGULATION

"When it comes to gossip, I have to admit men are as guilty as women."

— MARILYN MONROE

Picture the following scenario. You're in a meeting that is contentious. Perhaps there's disagreement about a project moving forward, a budget issue, a biased company practice, a new hire or a strategic decision. You make a suggestion that you think will help smooth out the process going forward and your boss immediately shoots it down. You're furious. The meeting continues but you sit in your seat, fuming about what happened. After the meeting ends, you head out to your car and run into a colleague. The two of you rehash the meeting and you talk about what a jerk your boss is for shooting down your idea.

Triangulation is a manipulation tactic where one person does not communicate directly with the person with whom they are disagreeing, but talks instead to a third person, thus forming a triangle. Perhaps you've experienced when two people are in conflict with each other and one of them chooses to bring in a third party by either 'processing' this conflict or trying to pit one individual against the other. The triangle does not help in solving the root problem. Typically, the issue is between two individuals in conflict and they're the ones best positioned, with the most insight into how the problem can be ultimately solved. Granted, there are times when a third party is absolutely necessary and helpful (sexual harassment, legal claims, mediation), but often including a third party is destructive and erodes the trust between the original two parties, making subsequent healing of the relationship more difficult.

Non-Triangulation (also called Direct Negotiation) means the two people in the conflict speak directly with each other and negotiate a mutually satisfying outcome. If they are open and using communication that helps them illuminate the real issues, they are more likely to reach a collaborative solution to their conflict.

To discourage the practice of excessively

DEFINITION
Triangulation:

a manipulation tactic where one person will not communicate directly with another person, but takes the message to a third person, thus forming a triangle.

Positive Triangulation:
intentionally talking behind the backs of colleagues in a positive way.

ACTIVITY!

Color the picture below.

involving an outside third party, adopting a policy of Non-Triangulation encourages a culture of Direct Negotiation. When the time comes that one of the people in the conflict approaches a third-party to pull them into the discussion, that third-party can very concisely, professionally and firmly redirect the triangulating party back to the person with whom they're having a conflict by saying "You two have the skills to work this out."

You and your team may consider adopting **Non-Triangulation** on a pilot or permanent basis and evaluate its usefulness in solving problems and building trust.

There is another practice called **Positive Triangulation**, which is intentionally talking behind the backs of colleagues in a positive way. Stephen Covey suggested that if you are talking about someone who is not in the room, PRETEND that they are present. One's language becomes gentler and more constructive by adopting this practice of pretend-presence. Positive-Triangulation will inevitably circle back to the person. It also has helped to instill norms for laudable behavior into the culture. If I talk about my colleague's resourcefulness and courage, I'm uplighting and promoting these features of her exemplary behavior. This will make her feel engaged and encouraged, and will also make me and others inspired to be resourceful and courageous. If your team's ultimate goal is to flourish and to help others flourish, Positive Triangulation is an effective means to that end.

"He was hitting her with all these really tough questions but she was like a ninja in there. And then she came up with this brilliant idea right on the spot. She saved the account for us. It was masterful."

The Good kind of Gossip

WORKSHOP NON-TRIANGULATION:

There was a particularly difficult conflict I had with another individual in my workplace. Another person was pulled into the situation which complicated matters.
In summary, this happened:

The cost of that situation was:

Now that I know about Triangulation, Non-Triangulation and Positive Triangulation, if I had a do-over button, I may have done this instead of how I originally communicated:

I may be Triangulating in this current situation:

I could do these three things to embrace Non-Triangulation with my team:

1.

2.

3.

I can think of three people about whom I want to Positively Triangulate.

PERSON	THE AMAZING THING I SHOULD TALK ABOUT BEHIND THEIR BACK

Explain what you think the difference is between seeking counsel and trash talk. How are the motives different? How are the tones different? How are the outcomes different?

Trash Talk Turnaround

by Sarah Colantonio & Kedren Crosby

ACT I TRIANGULATION

Dorothy and Arthur leave work at the end of the day.

Dorothy heads off to her car.

Arthur leaves.

Dorothy runs into Jack in the parking lot.

Dorothy vents her frustration about Arthur to Jack.

End of Act I

15. APPRECIATIVE COMMUNICATION

"We need to discover the root causes of success rather than the root causes of failure."
— DAVID COPPERRIDER

"We live in the world our questions create."
— DAVID, AGAIN

"Positive questions bring out the best in people, inspire positive action, and create possibilities for positive futures."
— DIANA WHITNEY

At 10 p.m., Kedren called me from South Carolina. "My flight was delayed so much that I missed my connecting flight to Philly. I won't be able to make it to the conference in the morning to give my presentation. I need you to do it."

After several heart attacks, we hammered out the details and I was set to speak. In the end, ten minutes before her talk was scheduled to start, she sprinted in. We co-presented and it ended up being kind of fun. But afterwards we said, what did we learn from this? How can we do better? I said, "When traveling, schedule a day between gigs in case of delays." She said, "Pack sneakers to be able to run faster in the airport." Appreciative Communication allows us the opportunity to focus on the positive. What do I do best? What can we gain from this experience? How can I improve on performance?

Appreciative Communication is born out of the field of Appreciative Inquiry which is an approach to organizational change based on strengths rather than on weaknesses. Organizations focus on a vision that's possible rather than analyzing the problem or talking about what's not possible. Based on the work of David Cooperrider, the father of Appreciative Inquiry, here are some principles to keep in mind:

▶ First, spend time talking about what gives you energy because the more you focus on your energy and your strengths, the more those increase.

▶ The second principle is to focus on what you want to achieve rather than what you don't want. You "raise your gaze" and focus on what could be, the possibilities.

▶ A third dimension of Appreciative Communication is discovering strengths. Be curious about what each other's strengths are and about the collective team strengths. Asking questions to get you to these strengths is a helpful form of appreciative communication.

DEFINITION
Appreciative Communication:
Talking about a vision that's possible rather than analyzing the problem or talking about what is not possible.

▶ One of the most interesting and engaging ways to embed identity into your organization is through storytelling. As you're discerning strengths, listen for pivotal stories that can be on heavy rotation. They stick in the minds of others and underline the kind of culture you want to have in your organization. You may ask your team "when are we our best?" and retell those stories to people who are new to the team so everyone has a sense of the team's superpowers. It builds momentum and also helps instruct people on the kinds of behavior that will be rewarded.

▶ Lastly, practice the "blameless postmortem." Think about how you deal with failure. There will be times when things don't go as planned and it's important to autopsy the failure in a con- structive way. Looking into the "cadaver" of that failure means getting serious about what went wrong and asking, "what happened here, so the next time this occurs, we can do it differently?" Examining failure in an appreciative light brings attention to the process, the sequence and guides us to improve.

Use these tools of Appreciative Communication and you will find that this positive light will give you greater effectiveness in accomplishing what you want to accomplish. You'll also have more joy, organizational well-being and deeper employee engagement along the way.

WORKSHOP APPRECIATIVE COMMUNICATION:

Asking questions of others opens them to positive possibilities while also empowering them to process and problem-solve. What is an area of my current work where I want to help others discern, discover and dream?

What question(s) can I ask of others that will enable them to recall and relive a time of strength on my team?

How can I retell, animate, repeat, relive these appreciative stories in ways to ingrain new employees with my team's identity.?

The superpowers of each of my teammates are:

My own superpower is:

When I think of my biggest career failure, in what way am grateful for that failure because of the positive consequences that resulted?

How can I communicate to my team that each failure contains data to be mined for the enhancement of future successes?

Collaborative Communication

IN A STRIKING EXPERIMENT, the authors of *Radical Collaboration* illustrated how important collaborative communication is in our work and relationships. At a session on collaboration, they took some volunteers and separated them into two teams. For the exercise, they had the teams act as if they were cleaning crews being interviewed based on a demonstration of their cleaning abilities. The authors created a mess for the two teams to clean up. In front of the audience, the first team was told they were going to clean up to showcase their abilities as part of the interview process.

The first team looked at each other before lethargically picking up paper and straightening chairs. One sat in a chair and started reading the paper. Others found money on the floor and fought over it. They bickered if they even interacted with one another and they barely cleaned up the mess.

The second team came out and were given the same instructions. Clean up the mess as part of the interview process. Team Two immediately started to figure out how to break up the work and got to it efficiently. When one finished a task, she volunteered to help with something else. They were enthusiastic and thorough. They also found money on the floor but instead of fighting over it, put it in an envelope and put it on the table. They seemed to enjoy one another and even chatted with each other while they worked. They finished quickly and did an excellent job.

The audience was amused and said that obviously, the authors must have told Team One to do a bad job and Team Two to do a good job. Nope, the authors said, that's not what we told them. They pressed the audience for their ideas. Guesses included inequity in pay, one team was supposedly trained and another was not. One team was told they didn't like each other and the other team was

16: **CONVERSATIONAL TURN-TAKING**

17: **THE GAP**

18: **ORGANIZATIONAL CONVERSATION**

19: **KNOW YOUR CONFLICT STYLE**

20: **AUTHENTIC PERSUASION**

Collaborative Communication goes hand in hand with self-awareness.

told they did. Another obvious guess was, oh, you told one team to not be collaborative and the other team to be VERY collaborative. That in fact was also incorrect.

*"We told Team One that we were going to ask them to do a simple task they could easily perform in a few minutes, and that we were specifically not giving them any instructions about how they should do the task. They could do it any way they wanted to. The only instructions we gave them was about how they felt about themselves. We said we want you to feel **insignificant, incompetent** and **unlikeable**. These feelings were not about the task, but only about how they felt about themselves.*

*We gave the same instructions about the job to Team Two; however, we told Team Two we wanted them to feel **significant, competent,** and **likeable.**"*

Collaborative Communication goes hand in hand with self-awareness. For it to really work, we need to have a healthy relationship with ourselves. By utilizing the other dimensions of communication that we've covered so far; Mindful, Emotionally Intelligent and Psychologically Safe communication, we can use that as a foundation for Collaborative Communication.

Collaborative Communication requires a bidirectional exchange of information to harness the collective brilliance of a team. Collaborative Communication also means we exercise assertiveness and provide clarity, are willing to state what you want as well as offer curiosity and discernment about what the other party wants. True collaboration melds the interests of the self and the other together to craft a mutually satisfying outcome. Collaborative Communication seeks to build cohesion that allows for dissent so that teams may have the broadest perspectives and most creative ideas.

16. CONVERSATIONAL TURN-TAKING

"The perfect metaphor for teams is a see-saw, not a sports team."

— EDGAR SCHEIN

The practice of Conversational Turn-Taking might conjure a hippie image of chilled out folks using a talking stick around a campfire, but it is effective around the conference table, or the dinner table. And it doesn't require an actual talking stick.

Google's Project Aristotle examined what makes teams extraordinary. Across the board, there was an even amount of input in conversation by all the team members. No one person dominated discussion. Everyone had the opportunity and was expected to share equally.

Charles Duhigg wrote specifically about Conversational Turn-Taking in his article on Google's Project Aristotle:

"As the researchers studied the groups, however, they noticed...members spoke in roughly the same proportion, a phenomenon the researchers referred to as 'equality in distribution of conversational turn-taking.' On some teams, everyone spoke during each task; on others, leadership shifted among teammates from assignment to assignment. But in each case, by the end of the day, everyone had spoken roughly the same amount. 'As long as everyone got a chance to talk, the team did well,' Woolley [lead author on a related study] said. 'But if only one person or a small group spoke all the time, the collective intelligence declined.'"

Conversational Turn-Taking results in several positive outcomes, not least of which is better team performance.

Conversational Turn-Taking results in several positive outcomes, not least of which is better team performance. Another benefit is better employee engagement. Many companies wonder how to instill motivation in their workers but an organic way to achieve this is to have everyone involved. Members are more likely to be engaged if they have skin in the game, if they had a part in implementing a new idea or plan. If our name is on something, we care about what happens to it. There's more ownership. And if that's the expectation in a team, that everyone has to contribute, then everyone is working harder to come up with the best possible ideas, the greatest way to achieve something, and the simplest most beneficial solution. Members are happier with outcomes that they were involved with, even if it means compromising and giving up some of their preferences.

The other benefit is it illuminates team members who might be unmotivated, overwhelmed, ill-repared or even burning out. If all members

ACTIVITY!

Color the picture below of Conversational Turn-Taking

are part of the process and will be heard from, and at every meeting one person is consistently noncommittal or without an opinion, that will be noticeable. And not in the good way. A notorious pitfall of small groups is the "moocher." This is a team member who gets the accolades and benefit of being in a productive group but doesn't do much to contribute. Conversational Turn-Taking highlights the moocher by either motivating them into working harder, getting help or spotlighting the fact that they are missing out on the collective achievement

At first, a leader might be the encourager of Conversational Turn-Taking. In a group of people, with all kinds of preferences, experiences, and personalities, a person might opt out of giving an opinion or sharing information. If someone is in a bad mood or insecure, they might refuse to share. Over time, as the team leader continues to encourage this norm, other team members will chip in and help make this the standard protocol for team meetings. It might even find its way into Ground Rules.

A *Wall Street Journal* reader wrote to Dan Ariely, the behavioral economics researcher and professor at Duke University, about a problem he was seeing in board meetings. Certain trustees were interrupting and taking over discussions. While the behavior had been called out, it was persisting. Ariely's reply was gold.

"A few years ago, my lab at Duke University designed a test: At a meeting, we connected all the participants' microphones to a screen that displayed

in real time how much each person was talking. It turned out that simply showing this information led to much more equal participation; in particular, the people who usually never talked started expressing their opinions. Until this technology is commercially available, you could try using a whiteboard or timer to keep track of how much everyone is talking. My guess is that will help the interrupters realize what they are doing and encourage the quiet ones to participate more."

While you might not use technology to utilize this practice, Conversational Turn-Taking requires many of the other Authentic Communication practices like Mindful Listening, the Pause Practice, and Self-Regulation. Also, if you assemble a team because you think they're brilliant and innovative and interesting, this is a vital practice. Leverage their brains and perspectives. The kinds of ideas that can emerge from many great minds playing off of each other is exciting to consider. And it's essential for collaboration.

> **The kinds of ideas that can emerge from many great minds playing off of each other is exciting to consider. And it's essential for collaboration.**

WORKSHOP CONVERSATIONAL TURN-TAKING:

How shared is the participation in conversation during team meetings?

Does anyone dominate the conversation?

Is there a person who never speaks up?

How can I enhance Conversational Turn-Taking on my team?

What will this require of me?

When will I start?

What benefits do I foresee by practicing Conversational Turn-Taking with my team?

Step 1 : Establish the expectation.

"Hey can you do this thing..."

Step 2 : Get buy-in.

"oh yes, sure, can!"

Step 3 : Depending on the outcome...

Expectation is met   or   Expectation is <u>not</u> <u>met</u>

Woohoo!

Address the gap and find out how they're going to close the gap.

17. THE GAP

"Treat those who are good with goodness, and also treat those who are not good with goodness. Thus goodness is attained. Be honest to those who are honest, and be also honest to those who are not honest. Thus, honesty is attained."

— LAO TZU

"If an offense come out of the truth, better is it that the offense come than that the truth be concealed."

— THOMAS HARDY, *TESS OF THE D'UBERVILLES*

Let's say that you have an expectation that your colleague would submit a report to you on Friday. You might say to her, "Hi Sarah, how are things? Can you give me that P&L by this Friday at 5 o'clock, close of business? Can you email that and by the way, it's the P&L that has the blue background." You're specific with her about which P&L you want. Then you say to her, "Does that work for you?" and she tells you, "Yes, absolutely that works for me."

Friday comes and goes.

Monday comes and goes.

There's nothing in your inbox.

It is Wednesday until you get a chance to talk to Sarah. You might be furious. Or disappointed. Or frustrated. The Gap is a practice that is perfect for such a scenario. The first part of The Gap is being clear on what your expectation is and in this example, you are. The P&L with the blue background, on Friday by 5 o'clock.

The conversation on Wednesday with Sarah might go something like this, "Sarah, I'm wondering, did you submit that P&L? I checked my inbox and I haven't seen anything. You may have submitted it but I haven't seen it." Then she could say, "Oh my goodness, I completely forgot about it." You can go on to describe this gap by saying, "Well, my expectation was that I would have it on Monday and it sounded to me like you were comfortable with that. It is now Wednesday and I don't have that P&L. We have a gap here. How are

we going to close the gap?" Talking about the gap and asking how we can close the Gap is helpful because it's not judgmental. It's collaborative. It's an inquiry and we know that questions can help people become curious rather than defensive. By describing this Gap and asking how we're going to close the Gap, you give her the opportunity to problem solve and she can suggest ways in which she wants to close the Gap. If she lands on a solution for closing the Gap that is satisfactory to you, encourage her to go ahead and close the Gap. You might want to ask her "Going forward, how can we make sure this Gap doesn't happen again?" Again, there is no judgment on Sarah that she is somehow failing you or that there's anything bad about her.

If this has happened a number of times, you might refrain from the collaborative "how can we close the Gap?" question and ask for her to be responsible by saying, "how are YOU going to close the Gap?"

Giving and Receiving Feedback

In order to use the Gap effectively, we have to be comfortable with giving feedback and also receiving feedback. Some organizations are proactive in training their managers how to give feedback, but almost no one trains their teams how to receive feedback. Let's talk about both.

First of all, it's helpful to have a self-check. Ask yourself, "Am I ready to give feedback from the right place?" For example, if I have been disturbed and I'm angry about some broken expectation, I might not be in the right place to give the feedback. I might need to get myself into the right place mentally so I am able to give the feedback from a constructive place, so I'm helping the other person become a better, more effective employee.

Secondly, ask the employee, "Are you able to receive feedback at this time?" You can word it however you would like but depending on the environment, this question might be suitable for some organizational cultures more than others. This is an empathetic question. You are trying to gauge your listener. It may be that they only have five minutes. It may be that their dog has died. Maybe they are not open to receiving feedback because they received some other bad news. If they say, "No, I'm just not able to receive feedback at this time," then you may say, "how about tomorrow?"

Third, use empathy. Put yourself in their shoes and feel what they might be feeling. It's a helpful tool because you will have better advice for them if you understand their point of view.

You might do a self-check to see how directive you have been in your request or instruction. In an effort to sound easy going and chill, I've issued directives in the form of questions or what sounds like a vague suggestion. This is not being clear about my expectations and so I have set myself up for disappointment unless my coworker has the rare ability to read my mind.

Next, pinpoint the problem. Too often when we give feedback, we're making generalizations about their behavior but we want to be as specific as possible so they will have clarity about how they can turn things around in the future. Using the Gap is helpful in pinpointing problems.

The last tenet to remember when giving feedback is to move forward. Co-create a path for forging ahead. You can use inquiry to ask them, "How do you plan to move forward? Knowing what you know now, what sounds like a good plan for you? How can I help your success?"

Receiving Feedback

While all of us receive feedback almost daily and sometimes hourly, few of us have been taught how to optimally receive this data. Often we approach receiving feedback with a fixed mindset which means we view the data as criticism. We believe that we are 'fixed' and a critique of performance is akin to a personal attack. While the feedback could help us succeed, we see it as negative and grow defensive. If, on the other hand, we've opened ourselves to being curious and grateful for the opportunity to grow in self-awareness, we can hear with new ears the information that might be helpful to us so that we can become a better version of ourselves. Receiving feedback requires setting your mind and your intentions to openness, curiosity and even exploration. Because we know our Authentic Self-Communication is sometimes inaccurate, feedback is the vital reality testing that many of us need. Think of a bit of feedback that you received from a courageous colleague, friend or boss who cared enough about you to share something that ultimately helped you grow. I will never forget my own incredulity when I was told that I was a catastrophizer (naturally I blew their feedback out of proportion).

Consider ways to adopt these five tips for yourself but also to share them with your team, your children and anyone you care about who is also seeking ways to become a better version of themselves.

Use the following exercise to practice using the tenets for Receiving Feedback.

ACTIVITY!

Find a partner for this exercise. For the first four statements, one of you will play the role of Giver. (And p.s., they are not using the tenets for Giving Feedback so brace yourself.) The Receiver will use the suggested tenet to respond to the feedback. For statements 5-8, switch roles so each of you gets a chance to experience both sides.

GIVING FEEDBACK

1. Self check: What is the purpose of the feedback? Am I ready to give it from the right place?
2. Ask, "Are you able to receive feedback at this time?"
3. Empathize
4. Pinpoint problems
5. Move forward

RECEIVING FEEDBACK

1. Be grateful for the opportunity to grow in self-awareness
2. Keep an open mind
3. Listen to understand, not to respond
4. Ask clarifying questions to get specific feedback
5. Analyze the feedback for usefulness and applicability

GIVER	RECEIVER
1. I feel like you aren't motivating your staff. They don't seem inspired.	Use Tenet ❸ from *Receiving Feedback* above to respond.
2. That meeting was longer than I expected.	Use Tenet ❹ to respond.
3. I spent three hours last night working on your evaluation so that I could give you detailed information.	Use Tenet ❶ to respond.
4. Has anyone ever told you that you talk too much during meetings?	Use any Tenet to respond.
5. I'd like to move you off this project. I think it's for the best for the company.	Use Tenet ❷ to respond.
6. You are absolutely worthless.	Use Tenet ❺ to respond.
7. I've noticed that you often don't make your deadlines for your monthly report.	Use Tenet ❹ to respond.
8. I feel like you didn't respect my work when you took credit for our project.	Use Tenet ❸ to respond.

WORKSHOP THE GAP:

The issues of accountability that come up in my office are:

I can be more explicit and clear in communicating my expectations (verbally, nonverbally, in writing, etc.) by:

I can use "The Gap" to help my team be more successful by:

In reviewing the best practices for receiving feedback, the ones I want to enhance for myself are:

How will I do this?

I will tell my supervisor/teammates that I'm working on those behaviors and ask them to help me improve.

(CIRCLE ONE)   **YES   NO   MAYBE   LET ME THINK ABOUT IT**

18. ORGANIZATIONAL CONVERSATION

"Just pay attention, then patch
A few words together and don't try
To make them elaborate, this isn't
A contest but the doorway
Into thanks, and a silence in which
Another voice may speak."

— MARY OLIVER, EXCERPT FROM THE POEM, *THIRST*

Think of a time when you felt like an outsider. When you were the minority. What did that feel like? Now think of what it would have taken for you to feel like you belonged? We've all felt like the outsider at one point or another in our lives. Some of us maybe much more than others. When you think of what would have made you feel like you belonged, for many of us it starts with being included in the conversation. If only your perspective was appreciated, or even considered, you would have felt seen and known.

Today, one of the reasons that diversity, equity and inclusion is a growing edge in many organizations and companies is because of lack of representation in our C-suites and in our board rooms. Creating more diverse and inclusive teams builds originality, intelligence and profitability.

Social psychologist, Heidi Grant, found that having diversity on a team makes a team smarter because they tend to *focus more on facts, process those facts more carefully than more homogeneous groups and they tend to be more innovative.*

Adam Grant, an Organizational Psychologist at the University of Pennsylvania, wrote a *Harvard Business Review* article which detailed his experience with how the U.S. Navy went about fostering originality by tapping into the perspectives of those who were normally either getting in trouble or simply did not follow the status quo:

"But in a matter of months, the navy was exploding with originality—and not because of anything I'd done. It launched a major innovation task force and helped to form a Department of Defense outpost in Silicon Valley to get up to speed on cutting-edge technology. Surprisingly, these changes didn't come from the top of the navy's command-and-control structure. They were initiated at the bottom, by a group of junior officers in their twenties and thirties."

This research is prompting a shift to a new way of leading companies. The old way of the CEO standing on high and cascading, uni-directional messages down to his direct reports is fading.

ACTIVITY!

Color the picture below of Organizational Conversation.

There is a better, more effective way to power your team, organization or company. Building flatter, more creative, engaged and diverse teams requires a powerful way of communicating. The good news is that you already know the basics.

Think about the ingredients of a magical conversation. What happens when you truly connect with another person through a meaningful conversation?

The Four Ingredients of Organizational Conversation

❶ **Intimate:** *trust, listening, getting personal*

❷ **Interactive:** *promoting dialogue, exchange, shift in communication channels*

❸ **Inclusion:** *brand ambassadors, thought leaders throughout*

❹ **Intentionality:** *leaders convey strategic principles not by asserting but by explaining them*

First, there is **Intimacy.** With Intimacy we promote trust, we utilize Mindful Listening and we get personal with one another. Being congruent helps bring about trust. Mindful listening shows attention and respect. Getting personal erases the barriers between the leaders and the employees.

In Michael Slind's article, *"Leadership Is a Conversation,"* he describes the case study of one CEO having "listening sessions" where people could voice issues. One festering issue that came up was that there was uneven compensation. Not only did he create the space to find out about the problem, but then he did something about it.

Getting personal can take many forms but every organization can figure out how it will work best for them. A company had executives talk honestly in short (not fancy) video clips about why particular values were meaningful to them. One value happened to be "diversity" and the company's finance executive talked about how he grew up in poverty in England and was teased for his accent and background. Slind remarked, "these

> **The old way of the CEO standing on high and cascading, unidirectional messages down to his direct reports is fading. There is a better, more effective way to power your team, organization or company.**

unadorned stories make a strong impression on employees."

Not only are conversations intimate, they're also **Interactive.** In a company where Organizational Communication is practiced, the CEO isn't standing on a stage with a microphone proclaiming their message. It's about dialogue, exchange and even adjusting the communication channels so they are bi-directional. Interactivity could mean promoting dialogue by utilizing other Authentic Communication practices like the Check-In and Check-Out or The Platinum Rule. Asking each other "What do you want?" is a powerful way to get in touch with one another when you are on a team.

Inclusion is the third ingredient. Brand ambassadors come from everywhere in the organization. A thought leader may use social media and email to promote their ideas using their influence rather than authority. Opening up the dialogue means everyone's voice is heard and everyone has something to offer. It can range from making sure the quiet person in a meeting gets a chance to share (Conversational Turn-Taking) to providing an open platform for employees to contribute ideas (at Work Wisdom LLC, we use the application Slack).

Inclusive communication requires that leaders and teams are both self-aware and skillful in making colleagues truly feel that they belong. Inclusive language requires learning how words foster meaningful respect and acceptance.

Lastly, **Intentionality** is important for a meaningful conversation. A leader shares the reasoning behind a decision or strategy to o gain the input and perspective of others. As Slind notes:

> *"Conversational intentionality requires leaders to convey strategic principles not just by asserting them but by explaining them—by generating consent rather than commanding assent. In this new model, leaders speak extensively and explicitly with employees about the vision and the logic that underlie executive decision making. As a result, people at every level gain a big-picture view of where their company stands within its competitive environment."*

Mindfully applying these ingredients in your organization can lead to transformation. When people feel like they belong and are committed to the vision, the winning aspiration, of their team or company, they can tap into the best of themselves, their creativity, their generosity, the energy and their genius.

WORKSHOP ORGANIZATIONAL CONVERSATION:

How can my team and I authentically communicate with more: (concrete ideas)

INTIMACY

INTERACTIVITY

INCLUSION

INTENTIONALITY

The ways in which my organization is still hierarchical, cascaded and unidirectional are:

I want to leverage the techniques of organizational conversation to become a more powerful thought leader in my organization in these ways:

ACTIVITY!

Color the picture below about managing conflict. Think about where you fall on the grid.

19. KNOW YOUR CONFLICT STYLE

"I'd agree with you, but then we'd both be wrong."

— UNKNOWN

"Conflict is productive."

— PATRICK LENCIONI

One of us grew up in a house that couldn't handle conflict. On one side, she had fiery Scottish DNA and deep generational, cultural norms for rebel-rousing. On the other side were famous white-knucklers, German, tight-lipped avoiders. These clichés don't do justice to the complexities and magnitude of how much they didn't deal with conflict. They struggled deeply as a "team" because they didn't understand the nature of managing differences, their own style or each other's. And they certainly didn't celebrate each other's ways of managing differences. She figured that being alone in her room avoiding the battles, especially with a bag of fresh Lancaster County potato chips was her destiny.

Kedren was almost 30 years old when she enrolled in a class that focused on organizational conflict management. For the first time she was able to examine her family through this lens. Learning her own way of managing differences vastly changed her life, her "teams" and her BMI, too. Self-awareness is like jet fuel for adopting new behaviors. A key behavior to predicting the effectiveness of a team is how they manage conflict. Conflict doesn't have to hurt a team but the way the team manages differences might.

There's a tool that helps us understand our predisposition to managing differences, called the **Thomas Kilmann Instrument.** Following is a version you can take a few minutes to complete.

We hope this information works as well for you and your team, even if your team is your family.

CONFLICT MANAGEMENT QUIZ

Directions: For each pair of statements, circle the one that sounds most like you.

1) A. Occasionally I hold back and let others figure out how to resolve the conflict.

B. I aim to focus on similarities rather than differences in views.

2) A. I like to resolve problems through negotiating.

B. I try to make sure everyone's concerns are addressed.

3) A. I know what I want and go for it.

B. I sometimes aim to make the other person feel better in order to end the conflict.

4) A. I like to resolve problems through negotiating.

B. I'm willing to give up my own views if it will help the other person feel better.

5) A. I always try to work together to solve problems.

B. I aim to avert uncomfortable situations when possible.

6) A. I do what I can to avoid tension.

B. I aim to convince others that I am right.

7) A. I stall in order to take some time to think about problems before approaching them.

B. I am willing to compromise when others do.

8) A. I know what I want and I go for it.

B. I aim to discuss problems openly so that they can be worked out right away.

9) A. Sometimes conflicts are better left not discussed.

B. I try to get what I want.

10) A. I know what I want and I go for it.

B. I like to resolve problems through negotiating.

11) A. I aim to discuss problems openly so that they can be worked out right away.

B. Sometimes I aim to make the other person feel better in order to end the conflict.

12) A. At times I keep my views to myself in order to avoid conflict.

B. I prefer a "give and take" solution to problems where both sides make adjustments.

13) A. If the other person can agree to disagree, I can do the same.

B. I make sure others know my views.

14) A. I share my thoughts and ask others to share theirs.

B. I aim to convince others that I am right.

15) A. I sometimes aim to make the other person feel better in order to end a conflict.

B. I aim to avert uncomfortable situations when possible.

First, let's examine the meaning of conflict. What do you dread the most about conflict? Many of us cringe at the mention of the word. When Kedren took her first Conflict Management course, her professor told her on the first day, "From here on out, we're not using the word, 'conflict', we're going to use the word 'difference' instead. We have too much baggage with the word conflict." A conflict or a difference is when you and another person have different wants or goals. It literally is having a difference.

Every conflict (or difference) you will ever encounter has two dimensions. On one hand there is the question of how assertive you're going to be in getting what you want. On the other hand, ask yourself how cooperative you are going to be in helping the other person get what they want. Within those two dimensions lie the five different ways we can manage conflict. We tend to utilize only one or two of the five but in reality we have five at our disposal and none of them are absolutely good or absolutely bad. It's situational. In learning about all five, you can finally take advantage of a larger repertoire for managing conflict.

First, let's examine the style for managing conflict known as **Accommodating.** When we utilize accommodating as a conflict management

style, we are not being assertive about what we want but we are being cooperative in helping the other person get what they want. Take for instance the example of starting a Work Wisdom podcast. Kedren very much wanted to start a podcast but Sarah did not. In the end, Sarah accommodated Kedren's wishes and we now have a podcast called, "The Behaviorist" that is all about organizational behavior. Sarah was less assertive about what she wanted but was cooperative (mostly) in helping Kedren get what she wanted. When we're accommodating, we sacrifice our own wants in order to satisfy the wants of the other person. It

THE FIVE MODES OF MANAGING CONFLICT:

❶ ACCOMMODATING: "We'll do it your way."

❷ AVOIDING: "I'm out."

❸ COMPETING: "We're going to do it my way."

❹ COMPROMISING: "I'll give it a little, if you give a little."

❺ COLLABORATION: "Wow, this is a better outcome than I imagined! We both got even more than we could have hoped for!"

might sound like rolling over but like the other styles, there are benefits to accommodating. For one thing, accommodating might be useful when you realize you are wrong or if the issue is more important to the other person. Sarah has admitted that as much as she didn't want to create the podcast, she's now glad we did.

Accommodating gives you a chance to help satisfy the wants or needs of another person and it will build goodwill between you. There are numerous positives to accommodating but it's important to notice if you are overusing that style. If you feel like a martyr or that you aren't ever heard, you might be overusing it. If you're underusing accommodating, you might notice that you have trouble building goodwill or you are viewed as unreasonable.

Next is **Avoiding**. Avoiding might sound bad because you are being unassertive and uncooperative, but it might simply be an instance of diplomatically side-stepping an issue, or postponing the issue until a better time. Maybe it's withdrawing from a threatening situation, or when you feel like there's no way that you're going to

win. A surprising benefit of avoiding is that it can empower your team to figure out the conflict for themselves.

Notice if you're overusing avoidance. Ask yourself, "Does the team have problems getting things done because they have trouble getting my input on the issue?" Perhaps you're not being sufficiently assertive in sharing your point of view or your interests. But if you're underusing avoidance, you might feel burned out, overwhelmed or you might even hurt people's feelings on a regular basis. Pay attention, because like the other styles, it has its place and is helpful, but over or underusing can cause damage.

Competing is a power-oriented mode. You are very assertive about what you want and uncooperative in helping the other person get what they want. When you're competing, you pursue your own concerns at the other person's expense. You use whatever power seems appropriate in order to win your position. Competing might mean standing up for your rights, defending a position that you believe is correct or simply trying to win. If it's an issue of ethics or even safety you might need to operate in this mode. Issues of justice, inclusion, equity and diversity sometimes require competing. "Speaking truth to power" is highly assertive and

"It's my way or the highway!"

less cooperative. It's useful to utilize competing as a style when you need quick, decisive action like an emergency. It is also helpful to go to competing when you have important issues with unpopular courses of action like cost cutting, and enforcing unpopular rules or discipline.

Be on the lookout for signs of overuse. This is not a style conducive to relationships. It's necessary to use but if you are overusing competing, you find yourself surrounded with "yes" people who are afraid to admit ignorance and uncertainties. Or on the flip side, you could be alienating those around you because you always insist on getting what you want.

If you are underusing competing, you might often feel powerless in situations, or you notice you have trouble taking a firm stand even when you see the need. If you think about those things and they sound true to you, you may actually be underusing this quadrant.

The fourth mode to investigate is **Compromising.** Years ago, when we took the Thomas Kilman Instrument, we found that we both were very low on our use of compromising. This is intermediate in both assertiveness and cooperativeness. In compromising, the objective is finding an expedient, mutually acceptable solution that just partially satisfies both parties. There's middle ground and you're splitting the difference. Maybe you're doing it their way one day and your way the other day. You concede in order to reach middle ground quickly. Successful marriages use compromise often. Even though we had both been teaching this for many years, it became more real for us when we were having conflicts and either going to competing or accommodating. When we learned that we weren't utilizing this particular style, we were impressed with how helpful it was in smoothing out issues we would normally disagree over. At first we were awkward, an issue would arise and we would start to argue and then remember, oh wait, what does compromising look like?

Compromise is the ideal mode to operate in when goals are moderately important but not worth the effort for the potential disruption involved in using more assertive modes. It's ideal when two opponents with equal power are strongly committed to mutually exclusive goals, often in labor-management bargaining, or when they want to achieve a temporary settlement of a complex issue. If they need to arrive in an expedient solution under time pressure or as a backup mode when collaboration or competition fails, using compromise works best.

"Let's just split the difference."

"Okay."

Signs of underuse might be when you sometimes find yourself too sensitive or embarrassed to engage in the give-and-take of bargaining. Without this safety valve of compromise, you may have trouble gracefully getting out of mutually destructive arguments and power struggles.

One sign of overuse would be that you're concentrating so heavily on the practicalities and the tactics of compromise that you lose sight of larger issues, or you're emphasizing bargaining and trading. This can undermine building interpersonal trust and interpersonal relationships that are very important for the long run.

The last style is **Collaborating.** There's a well known story about collaborating that helps clarify its meaning. A couple was fighting over the last orange in the house. They were both competing. He said, "My salary paid for the orange, I deserve the orange!" Shocked that he would pull such a sexist position, she said, "I had the foresight to buy the orange in the first place so I deserve it!" They went around and around. Finally, they went to compromise. They cut the orange in half and he took his half and peeled it, tossed away the rind and ate the fruit. She took her half, peeled

it, tossed the fruit in the trash (or composter) and started zesting the rind for the biscotti she was making for the next morning. If they had collaborated, he could have had all of the fruit and she could have had all of the rind. It was a missed opportunity. They would have had to say to one another, why do you want the orange?

Collaborating is both assertive and cooperative. You know what you want and are assertive in getting it. You know what the other party wants and you are cooperative in helping them get it. When collaborating, work with the other person to find a solution that is fully satisfying to you both. You dig into the issue deep enough so that you understand the underlying interests of everyone involved.

Collaborating is useful when you want to merge insights from people with very different perspectives on a problem or when you want to gain commitment by incorporating other's concerns into a consensual decision. A good example of our own collaboration happened when we decided we needed a new office. We could've gone to positions. For example, Sarah wanted something urban and modern and Kedren wanted something Parisian and grand. We almost came to fisticuffs by landing on certain spaces that were dramatically different, but then we decided to ask each other WHY we had in mind the visions we did. Sarah's underlying interest was in making our work feel fresh and innovative. Kedren's underlying interest was in

COLLABORATING
may take the form of:
▶ exploring a disagreement to learn from each other's insights,
▶ confronting and trying to find a creative solution when resources are limited

making our clients feel warm and comfortable. We ended up in a very urban 1924 skyscraper with décor that is overstuffed, velvet, furry and French. It works because we collaborated by satisfying our underlying interests. However, later we moved into an 1865 restored warehouse, so Sarah actually won the long game.

In the book, *Getting to Yes,* there are concrete steps to using collaboration.

▶ Separate the people from the problem. Get the people on the same side. Be easy on the people and hard on the problem. In this step, participants can literally sit on one side of the table and have "the problem" on a screen or chalkboard.
▶ Understand what people truly value. Don't get stuck on positions, see past those.
▶ Create objective criteria for evaluating the success.
▶ Design options that will satisfy interests and can be evaluated by the criteria.

While collaboration can give us satisfying results, it takes a lot of time and energy. Be mindful of the effort necessary and notice if your attempts to collaborate fail. It may be a sign of overuse. If you're underusing collaboration, you might notice it is difficult for you to see differences as opportunities for joint gain, joint learning, or joint problem solving? Perhaps others are uncommitted to your decisions or policies. They might feel their concerns are not being incorporated into decisions or policies. Maybe you didn't take the time to discern what their underlying interests are.

It's helpful when we know our own styles of managing differences for dealing with conflicts because we're able to be more mindful of our natural disposition. If my natural style is to avoid, I can work on being assertive and cooperative so that I eventually get to collaboration on a more regular

Learn your own conflict style. Ask questions of yourself. What are you gaining by using the style that you use? What are the potential costs? What could be the benefit of using other styles? Grow in self-awareness and see whether or not you begin to operate differently in the workplace when it comes time to manage differences.

CONFLICT MANAGEMENT QUIZ ANSWER KEY

1) **A.** Occasionally I hold back and let others figure out how to resolve the conflict. **AVOIDING**

B. I aim to focus on similarities rather than differences in views. **ACCOMMODATING**

2) **A.** I like to resolve problems through negotiating. **COMPROMISING**

B. I try to make sure everyone's concerns are addressed. **COLLABORATING**

3) **A.** I know what I want and go for it. **COMPETING**

B. I sometimes aim to make the other person feel better in order to end the conflict. **ACCOMMODATING**

4) **A.** I like to resolve problems through negotiating. **COMPROMISING**

B. I'm willing to give up my own views if it will help the other person feel better. **ACCOMMODATING**

5) **A.** I always try to work together to solve problems. **COLLABORATING**

B. I aim to avert uncomfortable situations when possible. **AVOIDING**

6) **A.** I do what I can to avoid tension. **AVOIDING**

B. I aim to convince others that I am right. **COMPETING**

7) **A.** I stall in order to take some time to think about problems before approaching them. **AVOIDING**

B. I am willing to compromise when others do. **COMPROMISING**

8) **A.** I know what I want and I go for it. **COMPETING**

B. I aim to discuss problems openly so that they can be worked out right away. **COLLABORATING**

9) **A.** Sometimes conflicts are better left not discussed. **AVOIDING**

B. I try to get what I want. **COMPETING**

10) **A.** I know what I want and I go for it. **COMPETING**

B. I like to resolve problems through negotiating. **COMPROMISING**

11) **A.** I aim to discuss problems openly so that they can be worked out right away. **COLLABORATING**

B. Sometimes I aim to make the other person feel better in order to end the conflict. **ACCOMMODATING**

12) **A.** At times I keep my views to myself in order to avoid conflict. **AVOIDING**

B. I prefer a "give and take" solution to problems where both sides make adjustments. **COMPROMISING**

13) **A.** If the other person can agree to disagree, I can do the same. **AVOIDING**

B. I make sure others know my views. **COMPETING**

14) **A.** I share my thoughts and ask others to share theirs. **COLLABORATING**

B. I aim to convince others that I am right. **COMPETING**

15) **A.** I sometimes aim to make the other person feel better in order to end a conflict. **ACCOMMODATING**

B. I aim to avert uncomfortable situations when possible. **AVOIDING**

WORKSHOP CONFLICT STYLES:

Tally the number of times you answered according to a particular style below:

_____ Avoiding

_____ Compromising

_____ Accommodating

_____ Collaborating

_____ Competing

Circle the style(s) you use the most. Are you surprised?

After you have absorbed the results and noticed what style of conflict management you use, notice if you would like to use another mode more often.

The mode I use most often is:

The mode I would like to use more often is:

The mode I would like to use less often is:

I will do the following to accomplish that:

At work I overly rely on a particular style of managing differences:

a. Why am I choosing this mode?

b. How is this serving me well?

c. What is it costing me?

d. What if I chose another mode?

FROM CONFLICT TO COLLABORATION: THE SCRIPTS

For this matching exercise, work through the triggers to find effective deescalation responses from the scripts on the right. What scripts do you use that work well?

TRIGGERS	SCRIPTS
That meeting was awful.	What was the best thing about it?
Our boss is evil.	I want to understand why you think this is true.
What is wrong with you?	I am asking you to cut me some slack right now.
You are completely wrong.	I'm glad we can share divergent views on our team. It will result in a better product.
Aren't you listening to me?	I want to focus on the solution, not the people.
Kedren isn't doing her work.	Is this really a problem with the structure or with the people?
You don't even care about our team.	We are all evolving.
Sarah is trying to get all the attention.	What could we gain from this if we instead satisfied all of our interests?
You're either for us or against us.	What do you think their underlying interest really is?
Let's just do it my way.	What's been their style of managing conflict in the past?
Sarah is greedy.	I don't want to take a position just yet. I want to lay our interests on the table first.

ACTIVITY!

Color the picture below about Inspiring Action.

20. INSPIRING ACTION

"We're persuaded when we feel we've understood something well enough to make up our own minds. And that makes all of us smarter, better people, no matter what side of the issues (or the table) we're on."

— KC COLE

The topic of influence and persuasion has fascinated human beings for thousands of years. And why not? It's worthwhile to understand how we are inspired by certain messages and yet completely unmoved by others. It's interesting to see how our efforts to inspire others to act seem to actually work sometimes. Equally compelling is why some efforts don't work at all.

Inspiring Action is using our ability to influence for good. We are not inspired by someone railing at us with their point of view. In fact, it makes us more steadfast in OUR perspective. Conversely, one of the biggest reasons we agree with someone else because their perspective matches the values that we personally hold.

There is a science to this concept of Inspiring Action. It doesn't happen organically. And it takes a deep understanding of ourselves and of those around us. When used effectively, it is powerful.

> **Inspiring Action is using our ability to influence for good.**

It's so powerful, we need to remember our ethical responsibility to use it wisely. While Elizabeth Holmes, the founder of the now defunct Theranos was very adept at influencing and persuading, she was a total fraud and led her investors to believe that her product actually worked when it did not.

Robert Cialdini's extensive and powerful research on the science of pre-suasion is very helpful when Inspiring Action. An important ingredient to Inspiring Action is the concept of Unity. Unity exists when we feel that we are part of a greater whole, whether that is a shared ideal or group identity. When we can tap into this feeling of unity and belonging, we can create positive change in our teams, organizations, communities and society.

The first stage to tapping into the sense of unity is illustrated in a study by researchers, Robb Willer and Matthew Feinberg. Participants were given the task of convincing the opposing political side of their perspective. Using the issue of same sex marriage, they prompted liberal participants to use the values held by their conservative counterparts to convince them that same sex marriage should be legal. Conservatives had to argue for more military spending. What happened? Most of the participants fell back on arguing from their point of view or basing their argument on their own values.

However, the researchers found if the message was framed in a way that matched the values of the listener, the likelihood of influencing their perspective rose significantly. If conservatives were invited to consider that gay Americans were proud and patriotic Americans who contributed to our economy and society, they were much more likely to soften toward legalizing same sex marriage. If liberals thought about military spending as a way to bolster disadvantaged Americans and provide reliable income, liberals were far more positive about the idea.

Framing a message to Inspire Action is hard to do because we hold our values so dear. It feels inauthentic to propose an idea using a value that we don't personally prioritize. First, consider your

own values. Using the exercise at the end of this chapter, rank them according to importance. This practice will illuminate how others might prioritize values much differently than you do and how that can impact your relationship. Have other people on your team or in your family prioritize their own values. Discuss your lists openly. It's also wise to notice the values you rank on the bottom of your list. This may explain why you don't connect as easily with people who rank your bottom value as their top priority.

Truly inspiring communicators practice mindful listening. With mindful listening, you don't have to agree with the other person. But you can still make sure you fully comprehend their point of view. Plus, you can use the time to ascertain what their values are based on the argument they present.

Not surprisingly, the practice of empathy is key for those who want to Inspire Action. With empathy, we imagine what it is like from the other person's experience. What might it be like to grow up the way this person has? To see the world the way they do? What is it like being that person? By

deeply considering the perspective and relative experience of the other, you are more capable of communicating in a compelling way to inspire action.

Other communication methods for inspiring action include adopting the six principles of influence according to Robert Cialdani as illustrated on the left.

Constructive emotional expression is another effective way to inspire others. Emotional expression involves openly expressing feelings both verbally and non-verbally. These messages can be conveyed through words, tone and volume of our speech, as well as the expressions on our face and our body language. Others sense these emotions both consciously and unconsciously. People who develop effective emotional expression are open and congruent in the emotional messages they send to others. When working to inspire the actions of our collaborators, consider how we might choose to constructively express emotions in order to move them forward. Not all inspiration comes from positive emotional expression of enthusiasm, optimism, hope and social responsibility. Sometimes we can move others to act when we express our concern about injustice, inequity or disappointment. Use emotional expression deliberately, authentically and artfully.

The important and groundbreaking work of the neuroscientist Dr. David Rock provides evidence of five primary and specific motivators for human beings. Knowledge of this powerful framework enables us to more effectively communicate to inspire action. Dr. Rock uses the acronym SCARF for the five brain-based motivators: Status, Certainty, Autonomy, Relatedness and Fairness. When attempting to move your colleagues or communities to action, consider how these five elements are sufficiently addressed into your communication. Status is the individual's perception of being considered better or worse than others. Certainty is determining the predictability of future events.

Autonomy is the level of control we feel able to exert over our lives (which is why micromanaging can inspire inaction). Relatedness is the sense of having shared goals and being part of the 'in crowd' with others on your team. Fairness is the sense that we are being respected and treated fairly in comparison to others. Fairness is a biological reason which underscores the vital importance of addressing inequity in our workplaces. Once we understand the power of addressing these five SCARF elements in our communication, we can be more effective in collaborating in ways that are helpful and generative.

And finally, just like storytelling, there is a structure to messaging that leads to action. According to the researcher, Nancy Duarte, every single great communicator who inspired action throughout history has used a common structure to convey their ideas.

▶ At first, they establish "what is". The boring, the unappealing, the dangerous, the evil of how things are.

▶ And then compare it to what could be. The potential of what the world would be like without that boring, unappealing or even evil thing. They repeat that pattern again and again.

▶ They propose a call to action.

▶ And finally end with the new bliss.

From Steve Jobs, to Martin Luther King, to Abraham Lincoln, this structure goes across the board.

Now that you understand ways of communicating to Inspire Action, remember to first evaluate your motives. Also, take note of when you are influenced and inspired to act. These concepts, when put into action, will help you take your team to the next level.

WORKSHOP INSPIRING ACTION:

Directions: Prioritize the following according to the most important to the least import- ant to you. Number **1** is the most important and number **18** is the least important;

___ **Ambitious**
(hardworking and aspiring)

___ **Broad-minded**
(open-minded)

___ **Capable**
(competent, effective)

___ **Clean**
(neat and tidy)

___ **Courageous**
(standing up for your beliefs)

___ **Forgiving**
(willing to pardon others)

___ **Helpful**
(working for the welfare of others)

___ **Honest**
(sincere and truthful)

___ **Imaginative**
(daring and creative)

___ **Intellectual**
(intelligent and reflective)

___ **Logical**
(consistent, rational)

___ **Self-respect**
(self-esteem)

___ **Loving**
(affectionate and tender)

___ **Loyal**
(faithful to friends or the group)

___ **Obedient**
(dutiful, respectful)

___ **Polite**
(courteous and well-mannered)

___ **Responsible**
(reliable)

___ **Self-controlled**
(restrained, self-disciplined)

My top 3 values are:

The way I learned those things about them was through:

My lowest 3 values are:

If I don't know their values and needs, what benefits would come from know- ing that?

The benefits to knowing the similarity/ differences in priorities between me and my team are:

How could I learn that information?

The values and needs of my customers/ clients/colleagues are:

RECAP:
THE 20 AUTHENTIC
COMMUNICATION PRACTICES

1. PARKING LOT

2. CONGRUENCE

3. THE PAUSE PRACTICE

4. MINDFUL LISTENING

5. AUTHENTIC SELF-COMMUNICATION

6. CHECK-INS, CHECK-OUTS

7. THE PLATINUM RULE

8. SELF-REGULATION

9. RICHNESS OF MEDIUMS

10. EMPATHY

11. GROUND RULES

12. ROUGH DRAFT

13. SPEAK-NOW-OR-FOREVER-HOLD-YOUR-PEACE-RULE

14. NON-TRIANGULATION

15. APPRECIATIVE COMMUNICATION

16. CONVERSATIONAL TURN-TAKING

17. THE GAP

18. ORGANIZATIONAL CONVERSATION

19. KNOW YOUR CONFLICT STYLE

20. INSPIRING ACTION

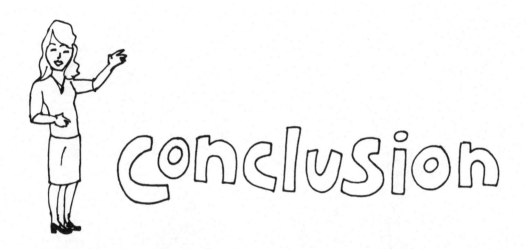

Conclusion

"Every great dream begins with a dreamer. Always remember, you have within you the strength, the patience, and the passion to reach for the stars to change the world."

—HARRIET TUBMAN

THEY SAY THAT YOU WRITE THE BOOK you need to read. This book grew out of our desire to be more Authentic Communicators ourselves. As with any healthy, helpful practice, (exercise, mediation, journaling, gratitude) it must be applied consistently to be transformative. While there is some benefit to simply learning the practices and adding the Authentic Communication vocabulary to your own, try selecting a few to use with deliberate intention.

When we work with teams, we ask them to select the tools which they believe will most significantly move the needle on the performance and well-being of themselves and for their teams.

Look over the list of twenty practices. Circle the three which you believe will most significantly improve your own performance and well-being.

Commit to experimenting courageously with them and weaving them into your communication.

Now look at the list again and consider your current team. Place check marks next to the three, if you adopted them would bring high performance and well-being to your team. If you have been working through this workbook with your team, now is the time to compare notes on which tools they're prioritizing to see if there are common themes.

It's exciting and fun to work with a team that does good work, that is creative, innovative, and makes things happen. These practices can help your team achieve that kind of greatness. So go forth and invent, problem-solve and make the world a better place using Authentic Communication!

Bibliography

Ariely, D. (2019, April 27). A Remedy for Big Talkers in Meetings. *Wall Street Journal*.

Baker, W. T. (2015). *Conversations at Work*. London: Palgrave MacMillan.

Cialdini, R. B. (2018). *Pre-suasion: A Revolutionary Way to Influence and Persuade*. New York: Simon & Schuster Paperbacks.

Duhigg, C. (2016, February 25). "What Google Learned From Its Quest to Build the Perfect Team." *New York Times*.

Dweck, C. S. (2016). *Mindset: The New Psychology of Success*. New York: Ballantine Books.

Edmondson, A. C. (2019). *The Fearless Organization: Creating Psychological Safety in the Workplace for Learning, Innovation, and Growth*. Hoboken, NJ: Wiley.

Fisher, R., Ury W., and Patton, B. (1991). *Getting to Yes: Negotiating Agreement without Giving In*. Yuan Liu/Tsai Fong Books.

Grant, A. (2016, March). "Build A Culture of Originality". *Harvard Business Review*.

Grant, H., & Rock, D. (2016, November 4). "Why Diverse Teams Are Smarter". *Harvard Business Review*.

Hitt, Miller, & Colella. (n.d.). Organizational Behavor (3rd ed.).

Hunt, V., Layton, D., & Prince, S. (2015, January). *Why Diversity Matters*. Retrieved from mckinsey.com

Murphy, K. (2020). *You're Not Listening*. Random House UK.

NPR Opinion 2.3.14 Tania Lombrozo "This Could Have Been Shorter". (n.d.).

Steel, J. (2007). *Perfect Pitch: the Art of Selling Ideas and Winning New Business*. Hoboken, N.J: Wiley.

Stein, S. J., & Book, H. E. (2011). *The EQ Edge: Emotional Intelligence and Your Success*, 3rd ed. Mississauga, Ontario: Jossey-Bass.

Tamm, James W. Luyet, Ronald J. (2020). *Radical Collaboration: Five Essential Skills to Overcome Defensiveness and Build Successful Relationships*. S.l. Harper Business.

NPR. (n.d.). The New Normal. *Invisibilia*.

Sarah

Kedren

Kedren holds a Master's degree in Policy Science from The University of Maryland, graduate level Certificates in Nonprofit Studies from The Johns Hopkins University in Baltimore, Conflict Resolution at Notre Dame and graduate coursework in Organizational Behavior at Harvard University. Her 25 years' workplace experience in all three sectors (for-profit, non-profit, government) fuel both her empathy and her practice which is rooted in authenticity, and appreciative inquiry. Kedren started Work Wisdom LLC, a practice dedicated to positive organizational behavior, in 2015.

Sarah has a Master's degree in Communication from The University of Tennessee. Since 2003, Sarah has taught Communication in the college classroom. Her areas of study are interpersonal communication, persuasion, public speaking, and group dynamics. A partner at Work Wisdom LLC, Sarah is a certified practitioner of Emotional Intelligence and Influence Style Indicator. She is also the creator of The Inner Office, a workplace cartoon on Instagram.

Kedren and Sarah are married and live with their dogs,
Lacy and Gracie in Lancaster, Pennsylvania.

WORK
WISDOM

"Work Wisdom helped clarify my leadership and professional evolution at an important time for me."

JESSICA KING, MBA
CHIEF OF STAFF, CITY OF LANCASTER, PA

"Work Wisdom's knowledge on work/life balance and emotional intelligence not only helped me become a better manager in the work place, but also improved my personal interactions outside of the workplace."

PATRICK BONNER
VICE PRESIDENT, ATOMIC DESIGN

"Organizing a mindfulness training was completely new territory for me. Both Sarah and Kedren offered great communication. Our first mindfulness training went so well that I was asked to set up another. Both groups absolutely loved Sarah and her teaching. I'd recommend Work Wisdom to anyone!"

STEVE ZIEGLER
SOCIAL MEDIA, THE WEBSTAURANT STORE

"The fact that Work Wisdom is a B-Corp is indicative of their commitment of integrating business and social values."

KEVIN MURPHY
PRESIDENT, BERKS COUNTY COMMUNITY FOUNDATION

"I can't speak highly enough about Kedren. She is a discerning listener and genuinely cares about helping others. Even a casual conversation with Kedren ends in revelation— in her subtle yet exacting way, Kedren has a knack for zeroing in on obstructions and empowering her clients to lift them."

KATHRIN THEUMER, PH.D.
ASSISTANT PROFESSOR, FRANKLIN AND MARSHALL COLLEGE

"Kedren and the Work Wisdom team enhanced our clinical leadership team's collective Emotional Intelligence, Collaborative practices, Growth Mindsets and Authentic Communication. These accessible, powerful and tangible deliverables have improved our team's performance and ability to care for patients. Kedren is a delight, a real joy to work with, and has some pretty fantastic jewelry!"

KIRSTEN JOHNSON MARTIN, D.O.
DO DIRECTOR OF OSTEOPATHIC EDUCATION AT PENN MEDICINE
LANCASTER GENERAL HEALTH